Praise for *Essential Healing For Your Spirit And Soul*

"We all need life coaches to help us to find the truth and heal our lives, minds, bodies and spirit. Essential healing can play that role for you. You don't need to be awakened by a disaster. Let the wisdom of others be your guide. Read on and find your way."

Bernie Siegel, MD
author of The Art of Healing and A Book of Miracles

"This timeless book hijacked my heart and invited me to commence what became a profound journey. As I began the book I hoped that each chapter would seamlessly weave into the next, gently expanding the path created by its predecessors. It did not disappoint! Each story was a gentle turn of the kaleidoscope of compassion with unique facets just as beautiful and brilliant as the last. Most importantly, it reacquainted me with the common threads we share with each other and with all beings and how that Sacred Oneness is our true spiritual salvation. This timeless gem is filled with practical tools guaranteed to enrich our lives! It is a permanent resident of my library!"

Dr. Kris Lecakes Haley
Department of Humane Religious Studies, Co-Chair
Emerson Theological Institute

"It was a pleasure to review Essential Healing For Your Spirit And Soul. I felt that the words just jumped off the pages to me. It warmed my heart to hear I could help myself by; Making a decision to keep an attitude of gratitude, Being present to Divine LOVE, Making a place to access Sacred Stillness...and so much more. I just want to soak it all up and I am sure that there are many other people who do also."

Michelle (Shelly) Ranney
Reiki Master, East Hartford, CT

"This book transforms the way we view life. Healer, heal thyself is how I would describe the writers in this book. We are all a healer, and we can all heal with the grace and power of a higher Source than our very own being. We all have this power from within. It is given to all indeed. And these authors without a doubt know how to find it, explore it and share it with the world."

Darcie Beyer
Co-author in Strengthen Your Wings 3-book series

Essential Healing For Your Spirit And Soul

20 Spiritual Practitioners Share Wisdom and Inspiration to Create Life-Changing Transformation and Healing

Compiled by Diane E. Hayden, PhD
Foreword by Bernie Siegel, MD

Natural Nutmeg Press, LLC
Avon, CT

ESSENTIAL HEALING FOR YOUR SPIRIT AND SOUL

20 Spiritual Practitioners Share Wisdom and Inspiration to Create Life-Changing Transformation and Healing

Compiled by Diane E. Hayden, PhD

Foreword by Bernie Siegel, MD

Natural Nutmeg Press, LLC

Avon, CT

Copyright ©2017 by Diane E. Hayden, PhD
Natural Nutmeg, LLC
53 Mountain View Ave. , Avon, CT 06001
www.naturalnutmeg.com

ISBN: 978-0-9912600-5-8 (softcover)

Jacket & Interior Design by Chris Hindman.

Essential Healing for Your Spirit and Soul is available for bulk purchase, special promotions, and premiums. For pricing contact publisher@naturalnutmeg.com.

Publisher's Cataloging-In-Publication Data
(Prepared by The Donohue Group, Inc.)

Names: Hayden, Diane E., compiler. | Siegel, Bernie S., writer of supplementary textual content.
Title: Essential healing for your spirit and soul : 20 spiritual practitioners share wisdom and inspiration to create life-changing transformation and healing / compiled by Diane E. Hayden, PhD ; foreword by Bernie Siegel, MD.
Description: Avon, CT : Natural Nutmeg Press, LLC, [2016]
Identifiers: ISBN 978-0-9912600-5-8 (softcover)
Subjects: LCSH: Spiritual healing. | Spiritual life. | Self-actualization (Psychology) | Change (Psychology)
Classification: LCC RZ403.S65 E87 2016 | DDC 615.852--dc23

DISCLAIMER NOTE TO READER

Although the author and publisher have researched all sources to ensure the accuracy and completeness of the information contained in this book, we assume no responsibility for errors, inaccuracies, omissions or inconsistencies. Any inaccurate characterizations of people, places or organizations are unintentional.

The information and procedures contained in this book are based on the research and the personal and professional experiences of the writers. This book has been published for information and reference uses only, and not for use as, or as a substitute for, diagnosis or treatment of any health problem. Neither the publisher nor the authors are engaged in rendering financial, health or other professional advice or services to the individual reader. If you require such advice, you should seek the services of a competent professional. Nothing in this book is intended as an express or implied warranty of the suitability or fitness of any service or product. The reader wishing to use a service or product discussed in this book should first consult a specialist or professional to ensure suitability and fitness for the reader's particular needs. Neither the authors nor the publisher shall be liable or responsible for any loss or damage arising from any information or suggestion in this book. The names of all clients mentioned in this book have been changed.

This book is dedicated to those who have helped us on our journeys and to those who are beginning their own journey of transformation toward more happiness, purpose, and fulfillment. Know that the first step begins with a thought...that you can do this... and ends with the belief...that you have already accomplished it.

Table of Contents

Chapter 12

Healing is Possible
Karen Lemieux, LCSW

Chapter 13

Strive for Five:
The Path to Successful Self-Healing
Andrea Frasier, RMT

Chapter 14

My Hands Led Me Here
Dan Lupacchino, LMT

Chapter 15

Discovering Mana: The 7 Essentials For Healing
Lauren Brandstadter, LMT

Chapter 16

Wellness From Within
Jill Myruski, LMT

Chapter 17

Creating a Healthy Body
Cynthia Haas, LMT

Chapter 18

Happy Feet, Happy Body

Chapter 19

Putting Myself First

Chapter 20

Coming Home with Yoga

Foreword

Your Potential for Self-Induced Creation and Healing

Bernie Siegel, MD

Our creator has built survival mechanisms into all of God's creatures. Bacteria can alter our genes and resist antibiotics. We cut our finger and a band aid covers the wound as it heals. People who develop and recover from life threatening illnesses, when doctors believe they are hopeless, are called spontaneous remissions or miracles. I have learned that they are not spontaneous or miraculous, they are self-induced. When you love your life and body you create an internal environment that chooses life and enhances healing. It is known scientifically as epigenetics. Friend and scientist Bruce Lipton said, "My personal identity signal is received by each of my cells endowed with the unique set of 'Bruce' self-receptors. My physical body is like a TV, the 'spiritual broadcast' representing the Bruce Show is an eternal, energetic element of the environment."

Monday morning is an example of how our life affects us, as it has the highest disease rate of any day of the week. So how do we induce healing and connect with the potential to heal that the Creator has given us? I can't help but think of a comment from Ernest Holmes and Religious Science; "What if Jesus was the only normal person who ever lived?" To do this we need to use our minds as remote controls and choose the spiritual channel to tune into and then demonstrate and live it with our bodies just as the TV screen reveals the program tuned into.

God is never the problem but religions and the guilt, shame and blame associated with them by some can be. I was called satanic and occult by a minister because I used meditation and guided imagery and he believed Satan could take over your images. When asked in his newspaper column, "Does God want me to have cancer?," Billy Graham answered, "Not necessarily, but God could use the cancer to bring you back into God's spiritual world." Pope Leo Xll, in the 1800's told Catholics not to vaccinate themselves against smallpox because, "Smallpox is a judgment of God – vaccination is a challenge toward Heaven." A vaccination would eliminate you as a child of God. Folks, remember as Maimonides said, a disease represents a loss of health, so look for what you or those you care about have lost and help them to find it. Centuries ago he also said, "If people took as good care of themselves as they do their animals, they would suffer fewer illnesses."

Solzhenitsyn, in his novel "Cancer Ward," speaks the truth because of his life experience. He writes about the physiology of optimism. The men are sitting in the cancer ward when one comes in and says, "I found this book in the library. It says here there are cases of self-induced healing. Not recovery through treatment but actual healing." And it was as though self-induced healing fluttered out of the great open book like a rainbow colored butterfly for everyone to see and they all held up their foreheads and cheeks for its healing touch as it flew past.

Why a rainbow colored butterfly? It contains all we need to know in symbolic form. Every color has meaning and when you create a meaningful and orderly life through changing and becoming your authentic self, healing occurs, physically, emotionally and spiritually. The rainbow represents your life in rhythm and harmony and the butterfly is the symbol of change and transformation which leads to a rebirth and healed life.

An example: I knew a woman who had cancer of the pancreas and was given no hope by her doctor. She went home to get her life in order. Over a month later she returned to her doctor's office and an examination revealed no sign of the cancer which was so large it could be felt in her abdomen. When I asked her to tell people what she did she said, "I left my troubles to God." Wish we could all do that before we get to the point when we feel our lives are threatened and time limited. I must add the best hospices have graduations and discharges when they help people do the same thing as part of their process of healing and compassion.

A landscaper I operated on for cancer, refused further treatment to go home and make the world beautiful before he died. I learned he didn't die when he came back to my office six years later for me to fix a hernia he developed while beautifying the world. He lived into his nineties with no sign of cancer. One woman who got so busy doing what she loved sent a letter to me describing all the joyful changes made in her life. She said, "I didn't die and now I'm so busy I'm killing myself. Help, where do I go from here?" When you love your life and body amazing things can happen.

I believe the reason we sleep is to dream. God and all of creation speak to us in dreams and images. Our dreams and drawings speak of the past, present and future. I, and people I know, have had dreams, or done drawings, which told them about their body's state of health and have been used to make a diagnosis. In one dream a dark skinned woman with an accent told the dreamer she had a lump in her breast. The woman turned out to be her hospital doctor who diagnosed the cancer. I have diagnosed patients from their drawings too. I feel that past lives are really the consciousness of those whose lives preceded ours now impregnating our minds and affecting our lives, talents and more. I speak from experience because I had a near death experience as a four-year-old choking on a toy and as an adult went into a trance when a friend asked me, "Why are you living this life?" She was trying to get me to slow down. Well the trance and past life experience was incredibly therapeutic and informative about me and my life.

Our physical brain and mind is also very powerful and our bodies believe what the mind conceives. Patients have side effects of treatments they are going to receive while they are on the way to the doctor. Also when medical errors have been made and placebos given, doctors did not realize they weren't treating people because the patients all acted as if they had side effects and benefits of the treatment they thought they were getting. We are given many gifts by our Creator but they need to be used properly and to enhance our health and healing and not cause self destruction.

The key theme to communicating with God or animals is the still pond and quiet mind. I hear a voice speaking to me which has made a very significant impact on my life because I listen to what the voice tells me. It happens when I am mentally still. I also have a medium friend, Monica, who regularly calls me with messages from my dead parents and others. As an example years ago, Monica told me I was going to write a book. I told her that would never happen. I am an artist and the only time I received a C in four years of college was in creative writing. I am now the author of fourteen books.

We are all God's children literally made of the same stuff. There is nothing else we could be created from except the loving, intelligent, conscious energy which is what God is all about. Our planet has been around for billions of years. Creation is an ongoing process and in stages we create what will allow for a higher state of being. Oxygen was created by our predecessors for us to live with.

We become a part of God when we die and our consciousness returns to its source. For me death is a graduation and like graduations it is a commencement. Two words I play with to keep me aware are Guidance and Slices. The former is interpreted as: God you and I dance, and the latter what God represents: Spirit, Love, Intelligence, Consciousness, Energy, and Soul.

So quiet your mind and all will be made clear to you and live and believe in what you experience and do not let beliefs and words limit your lives. Explaining life is impossible. Even Einstein said either everything is a miracle or nothing is. My feeling is everything is and I live in awe and wonder and gratitude.

One last point I have struggled with. If God is all I said God is, then why didn't God make a world free of all the problems and difficulties we need to live with and experience? At a past meeting of the Board of Directors of Heaven, where I am an outside consultant, I asked God, "Why didn't you make a perfect world?" God's answer was, "Bernie, a perfect world is not creation. It is a magic trick. You are all here to live and learn." I realize now that life is a school and full of tests, but if we raise our level of consciousness by learning the future, life will be much more like the Garden of Eden.

If you could be God for a day it shouldn't be because you want to fix something because perfection is not the answer. Being God would allow you, as the Baal Shem Tov said, to understand why. You can ask for me to pray for world peace and not for your personal needs.

The ultimate answer is for us to become a love warrior and use love as our weapon in life and all its conflicts. There was the word and the word was with God and the word was God. Replace the word with consciousness in that sentence and it explains life.

I will add that I think humor is vital for our survival too. Our lives are stored in our bodies and the wounds take their toll. As Jesus said, If you do not bring forth what is within you it will destroy you. If you bring forth what is within you it will save you. We need to become authentic. He who seeks to save his life will lose it, but he who is willing to lose his life will save it. Yes, eliminate the untrue self and be born again.

And to conclude with another question I asked of God related to Adam and Eve. God said that when He told Adam He was going to provide him with a lovely mate Adam asked what it would cost him and God replied, "An arm and a leg." Adam responded, "What can I get for a rib?" and the rest is history. I can tell you though that when love is involved you will find as I and Adam have that I would rather be out of the garden with her than in it without her.

For many, Dr. Bernard Siegel-or Bernie, as he prefers to be called-needs no introduction. He has touched many lives all over the Planet. In 1978, he reached a national and then international audience when he began talking about patient empowerment and the choice to live fully and die in peace. As a physician who has cared for and counseled innumerable people whose mortality has been threatened by illness, Bernie embraces a philosophy of living and dying that stands at the forefront of the medical ethics and spiritual issues our society grapples with today. Read Bernie's regular blog posts on his website where you will also find his books, articles, and CDs: www.berniesiegelmd.com.

Chapter 1

Raising Your Vibration to Create the Life You Desire

Jackie LaBarre, RScP

As a young child, I realized that all was possible, I could be and do anything I put my mind to being. By my teenage years, that belief was pushed aside and buried as life happened and many voices convinced me otherwise. Life went on until I began to awaken to a power that was greater than me; a benevolent, loving Spirit that wants only good to unfold in my life. At that point, my conscious spiritual journey began. Before my spiritual awakening, life just seemed to happen with no rhyme or reason; it felt that life was full of difficult times to be endured until it was all over. However, there were times when life did seem to flow evenly and effortlessly. I did not realize that there was a connection between my experience of life and how I was thinking.

In my forties, life finally crashed around me when my marriage fell apart, my children began acting out and I became a slave to alcohol. Through loving, supportive family members and friends I found my way out of the hell my life had become, entered recovery and began my spiritual journey and the awakening of my consciousness. Little did I know the huge impact that was to have on my life and the lives of those around me.

Throughout this journey, I have explored many paths of religion and spirituality and from each I was given gifts of wisdom, knowledge and insight into how this Universe works through spiritual laws. These laws work as reliably as the physical laws we all know, such as gravity. When I was introduced to a philosophy of living life called, 'Science of Mind' by Ernest Holmes, my life changed forever. Science of Mind is the study of Life and the nature of the laws of thought. I have learned that we live in a spiritual Universe; that there is a Power greater than any human and some call this Power, God, which is in, through, around and for us and there is nothing against us. This Power is what animates all life in the Universe because it is the One Life. Each of us is an individualized expression of this One Life and because of this deserves the life we would love to live.

Our thoughts are creative and it is the tendency of our thoughts which shapes our life experience. There is an ancient wisdom which states, "As above, so below; As within, so without." In other words, what we see in our outer experience is a reflection of what is inside of us, our predominate thoughts and it is these thoughts which create our life. If we can change the focus of our thoughts, our life will change.

When I was introduced to this idea, I was angry. How could I be responsible for the chaos in my life? As I looked back through the years, I realized that there times when I could quell the many voices of fear, doubt and worry and when I did, my life improved. Maybe there was something to this ancient wisdom! Ernest Holmes said, "Change your thinking, change your life." Wayne Dyer said, "When you change the way you look at things, the things you look at change." This is spiritual law, what many of us have come to know as the Law of Attraction. When we can change where we put our attention (worry, doubt, and fear versus what is working, what I desire in my life) we can attract a different life! Consciously directing our thoughts, training ourselves to pay attention to what we are thinking, letting go of worry, doubt, fear and misbeliefs about ourselves, allows us to use spiritual Law to change our experience of life.

The Law of Attraction always works. It begins to appear it is working for us when we begin to work with it. All things in the Universe are created twice, once as an idea and then it becomes manifest in the physical realm. Defining what it is we want in our life is the key to using the Law of Attraction. Without this, life happens by default. Our desires in life are our soul expressing what we are worthy of having and we need to get ourselves out of the way by shifting our thoughts to focus on those desires. When we define what it is we want in life and begin to move in that direction, we raise our vibration to what we desire, creating a container for the energy of life to fill and we begin to bring opportunities into our experience. As Ralph Waldo Emerson said, "Once you make a decision, the universe conspires to make it happen." Our thoughts can be our biggest ally...or out biggest obstacle to creating the life of our dreams. Thoughts of fear, worry, and doubt can impair the unfoldment of what we want. Harboring these thoughts sends mixed messages into the Universe and we get mixed results.

There are many spiritual tools to use to assist in changing our thinking and keeping it on track toward what we want, one of them is the use of affirmations. Affirmations are powerful statements of what is desired stated in the present tense and a positive voice, as if the desired condition was already in existence. Using affirmations is a beneficial way to retrain our thoughts throughout the day. If a more joyous, peaceful life is desired, affirmations like these can be repeated during the day:

I am a joyful, happy person.
My life brings me joy every day.
I deserve a peaceful, joyous life.
I choose to be peaceful.
It is okay for me to choose joy and peace.

As a Spiritual Practitioner and DreamBuilder Life Coach, I work with people to determine their life purpose and define their dream. Bringing the dream into fruition is like planting a garden. Once the dream is defined, the seeds have been chosen for your garden. Changing your negative thoughts and taking actions which support the dream is like preparing the soil, adding rich nutrients, and weeding the garden to allow its growth.

There is an affirmative prayer called Spiritual Mind Treatment that accelerates the preparation of the soil for whatever is your desire. This prayer acts like a laser cutting through the seeds of doubts and fears, creating a container into which Life can flow easily and effortlessly allowing the dream to be fulfilled. Spiritual Mind Treatment is a five step prayer where each step raises one's consciousness to the vibration of the desire using affirmative statements similar to affirmations. The five steps are:

1. We recognize that there is One Infinite Power which is the One presence everywhere in the universe, the One energy from which all things are created.
2. Having recognized this magnificent Power which created all, we unify ourselves with It by acknowledging that this Power is within us, It is the substance of all life and that we are Divine beings created by and from It.
3. We affirm our desire(s) with the feeling that it is already ours. We express those qualities of the Infinite Power which we want to embrace within ourselves which will raise our consciousness to that vibration. Just as an affirmation is positive and present tense, so are the statements in this step. We claim our desire.
4. Knowing this Truth, we express our gratitude and give thanks for that which we desire. It is this attitude of gratitude which opens our consciousness to receiving.
5. With gratitude, we release our word into the wisdom and love of the Universal Law knowing (trusting) that it is already done.

My personal experience using Spiritual Mind Treatment for myself and for my clients has been amazing. Once the prayer is done, the seed of desire is planted and the soil is prepped. We can then move confidently in the direction of our dream, weeding our thoughts as we go.

The following is a Spiritual Mind Treatment for physical health.

There is an Infinite Creative Power which is behind all life in the Universe. It is the One Life, that Life is God. That Life is my life now. It is this One Life that circulates through me, as me and animates my whole being. I am one with its peace and wholeness. In this Divine Life, there is no inaction only Right Action. There is no stoppage nor hindrance nor obstruction to its flow. Whatever may seem to be to the contrary is false, for I identify my physical body with the body of pure

Spirit. I open my mind as a channel for the realization of the Divine Presence. I affirm it and accept it. Nothing within me can deny or reject it. It is the pattern of God perfection within me which emerges as me. Quietly, I affirm and reaffirm these simple statements and they sink into my consciousness and become a habit pattern of thought that is no longer rejected or set aside. With complete conviction I accept that I am with the harmony, the perfection, and wholeness of the One Life. I am grateful to know this Truth and hold it in my heart. I release this Word into the Law of Spirit knowing it is already so. And so It is.

Let each of us become that which we desire. Let us allow our full potential for good to shine through and ignite the Spirit within ourselves and others.

Jackie LaBarre, RScP, is the owner of Conscious Healing Center located in Bethel, CT. As an engineer with a diverse background, she has worked at large corporations in a variety of management positions. In her leadership positions, Jackie developed her skills to listen deeply and help people find their true calling in life. After leaving the corporate world, she trained as a massage therapist and became the owner of her massage school. It was at this time she was introduced to the spiritual principles and practices which she used to create and develop her successful massage school. Jackie is now a Licensed Spiritual Practitioner with Centers for Spiritual Living practicing through the Connecticut Center for Spiritual Living and also a spiritual life coach in her Conscious Healing Center. She has recently become a certified Dream Builder Coach with Mary Morrissey's Life Mastery Institute. For more information, visit www.chctransformation.com or email: jackie@chctransformation.com.

Chapter 2

Integrating the Spiritual and Material Worlds

Enid Martinez, Certified Money Coach, CMC®

"The Heart is the Mine, Love is the Gold."

MIW (Master of Infinite Wealth)

I was born in Cuba, a beautiful island with a tyrannical regime, where material scarcity and repressed self-expression were prevalent. Everyone was controlled, we had to be careful of what we said or did or else we would be reported to the authorities. My experience with lack and limitation was daily. The environment rewarded excellence in academics and was conducive to competition. As a way to "fit in" and survive in a system that was rejecting my family for thinking different, I developed a strong belief that "knowledge is power," so I excelled in school, was very popular and did well at debate competitions held among schools. The intellect became my friend. I was highly driven and ambitious as I started nurturing a type-A personality.

When I arrived in the United States, the country of opportunities and freedom, I was challenged by a different language and culture. Integrating these differences at the beginning of my teen years was a very daunting task. However, whenever we experience challenges, the Universe also offers resources and support. We just need to be open to the possibilities. I received help from family members with school homework and assignments. I passed seventh grade and within one year, I was able to have a conversation without much effort. I was in the country of opportunities, and was determined to succeed.

The Unexplainable - My Early Teens

My earliest memories of having extra-sensory abilities date back to my early teens. I used to have dreams that would later come to fruition. I felt confused because I thought that by dreaming it, I would cause it to occur. I did not fully understand the symbolism of these dreams and only when the event happened was I able to make sense of them.

I also started, as many teenagers did, playing with the OUIJA board. What puzzled me is that I could run the OUIJA by myself. As soon as I touched it, it just took off. I was not forcing it, yet I had a sense, before the words were completed, of the entire message. How could this be possible? I eventually decided to stop using the OUIJA board. I was weary of what I could not understand, however, I was also curious to know more.

At the age of seventeen, I had my first out-of-body experience. I took a cassette of a meditation for Astral Travel. I was curious so I used my headphones and played it. Before I knew it I was flying among shrubs and felt very scared. I don't remember how I got back into my body and decided not to do something I could not understand. Once again my intellect was baffled, and was left with more questions than answers.

The dreams continued throughout my college years, until I decided not to have them anymore due to lack of understanding. So the dreams stopped, but I sensed that they would return some day. I loved Mathematics and after getting my bachelors in Math, I continued with my studies and got my MBA in Finance when women were just starting to get into a field that was predominantly male. I was still operating under the belief that "knowledge is power," and I was motivated to be financially independent and succeed.

Within a few years after grad school, I started working as an International Private Banker in New York City. I loved talking about money and educating and helping clients make investment decisions. I truly loved this job, it combined my language skills, math, money, travel and yes, psychology. As an International Private Banker, I could not help but wonder if I was already becoming a money psychologist. I would listen to my clients' relationship with money, their

8

fears, their beliefs, and observed their behaviors and money decisions. I was careful in offering financial products that they could understand and be able to stomach when markets turned downward.

Because of my great work, I was temporarily posted in Argentina. The first night in Buenos Aires, I had a dream that a Virgin appeared and told me that I was going to be okay, and not to be afraid. That is when the dreams returned. I was in my early thirties at the time. This was a renewed relationship with the unknown and a part of me that was destined to blossom. It was the beginning of a new phase of my life where the material/visible world and the spiritual/invisible world would collide but later integrate.

While in Argentina, I started taking "energy classes" at night. I began taking classes in Intuition/Psychic Development, reading objects with my eyes closed, reading people just by getting their names and age, reading others' emotions and bodies. I also took workshops on re-birthing, money, and Neuro-Linguistic Programming. I loved these courses, and I thought they were useful in my life. I just never imagined that I would become more involved in spiritual work and energy medicine. I loved my present job and had no intention of changing my life. I felt as if I was living a double life, a successful young International Private Banker during the day and a mystic at night. And never the two shall meet.

The Surprising Twists and Turns of Life

One day, during a business trip, I heard an inner voice that said, "Get ready, this is the end of your banking years." I was startled by this thought that came from a still depth. What happened within one year of this episode was a whirlwind of changes. The New York office moved to Miami, and I was asked to either move to the new branch or quit. I decided to quit the bank and return to New York. This decision was very difficult for me to make. I felt the winds of change coming but I still was not ready to give up my banking work that I loved so much. I refused to heed the spiritual calling.

As much as I tried to find a new job in this very specialized field of banking, I couldn't. I tried everything, even considering a lower position. Nothing worked, so I started temping and started getting nervous about my future. I had worked long and hard to get to where I was and was not ready to let it go. I wanted to have a similar lifestyle to the one I had before quitting the bank.

Resistance Leading to Illness

Simultaneously I was drawn to read many books on spirituality, however, I resisted changing careers. I began to get sick; I started having anxiety and borderline panic attacks. One day I sat on the kitchen floor and said, "You win, tell me what to do because I want to be well." I then physically felt angel wings wrapping around me. I was guided by this Angel to take certain steps to heal and to also start school. Within one month of following my "Angelic protocol to wellness," I healed. I started school to get a Doctorate in Energy Medicine as a Medical Intuitive. I finished all my required courses, and although I did not finish my Doctoral thesis, I learned all different modalities about energy healing, and I wrote a 355 page research paper on distance healing toward my thesis. While at school, I started having visions of Spirit Guides that seemed to be doctors. These Spirit Guides looked human but seemed to be different. They taught me how to do "etheric surgery." Etheric surgery is healing the Etheric Body, which is an exact replica of the physical but lighter. It also contains the chakras and meridians. I was taught how to repair the etheric body, and then these healings would then integrate into the physical.

Even though I learned a lot at school, I still questioned if this was what I would do for the rest of my life. I used to have a belief that money had no place within the spiritual arena, belonging more to the material world. There was a sense of separation between Spirit and materiality as expressed in this case through money. Even though I loved my spiritual work, I also loved money, and I would often experience confusion around where and how these two should ever meet; a question that I presently understand and integrate.

My healing skills have evolved with time, every session is different and requires being present to Divine Love and trusting what comes through. The healing is really about helping others connect to their own SOURCE of healing. My healing evolution continued as I would get visits from a Spirit Being called Master of Infinite Wealth. His message to all of us is that, "The Heart is the Mine, Love is the Gold." He teaches me about money from a spiritual-energetic perspective. We all have everything we need inside of us. Every answer to every question stems from LOVE. When we are very connected to that state of inner peace and love, things go smoother and miraculous things happen more frequently.

Coming Full Circle – The Integration Process

I love Energy Medicine. I now work more from a place of witnessing and guiding my client's own transformation by creating a safe, compassionate space for them to experience their own power. I love working with animals which bring me much joy.

After many years on a Spiritual journey where I had access to and learned from the Spiritual realms, I am presently experiencing a reintegration process of further merging these higher realms' teachings, insights and laws, with the material world. One powerful expression of the material world is money. I am presently guided to expand my healing work to address money. My present focus is offering money coaching services. Through my money coaching services I assist clients to discover their underlying unconscious limiting beliefs and patterns of behavior around money. Whether we want to admit it or not, money affects us all regardless of background and socio-economics. I enjoy guiding others to transform their relationship with money and with themselves so that they can live more fulfilling lives. It is said that money makes the world go round. I say love is, yet money is a very powerful tool of exchange that seems to affect all aspects of ourselves. We all have a unique relationship to money, as we explore and become more aware of this relationship, we can make more empowering choices and enjoy more financial freedom and wellbeing. Money is energy, and it shapeshifts to mirror our level of awareness.

It is interesting how my life has taken me full circle. In January 2012, I was guided to assist others in releasing and transforming the different expressions of fear and lack around money. It is no coincidence that I was born in a country where lack and tyranny were the order of the day. Money permeates the physical, emotional, mental and spiritual aspects of ourselves. By exploring our relationship with this powerful tool of exchange, we increase our awareness about ourselves. Understanding our money history and behavioral patterns allows us to address what is behind these attitudes and behaviors. Once we are aware, we can then incorporate an intuitively customized strategy to modify these behaviors and as a result experience more fulfilling lives.

Final Message

The material world is an extension and expression of Spirit therefore it is not separate from it. We all have gifts, talents and skills that are unique to each, and we bring them to this world as a contribution of our Divine-Human expression. We are here to materialize Divine expression. Everything in life has a reason to be, we need to trust that things always work out at the end. I love to guide and support others to connect to their inner knowing and transform their limiting circumstances, whether financial or otherwise, to a more fulfilling experience.

Enid Martinez is a Certified Money Coach (CMC)® and Spiritual Counselor. She is also a former International Private Banker. Enid skillfully integrates these disciplines into powerful tools to help others build more fulfilling lives. Enid effectively guides and assists others, through practical and simple ways, to become more aware about their relationship to money and themselves. Most importantly, she assists and guides others from a place of non-judgment to make changes in their lives and money behaviors. Her ability to see the full spectrum of a client's situation aids in getting to the root of a client's challenge and allows for true, effective solutions. Enid guides others to actively live the lives they dream and experience financial freedom. Enid's other passion is doing healing work with animals, both wild and domestic, including assisting with transitioning during their dying process. She also teaches classes on Spirituality, Intuition and Money. Enid received her training and certification from The Money Coaching Institute, a coaching training organization located in Northern California. She also completed 60 credits at Holos University Graduate Seminary in the field of Energy Medicine and Spirituality in which she has over ten years of experience. She earned an MBA in Finance from Rutgers University, and is certified in Basic Hypnotherapy. Enid can be contacted at enid@affluentawareness.com or visit her website at affluentawareness.com.

Chapter 3

Creating Phenomenal Relationships

Susan Lazar Hart, MFA

S imply by reading these pages, you are already on your way to creating a phenomenal relationship. So congratulations! You've chosen you. By choosing you, you are taking the first step to creating a relationship outside of the ordinary into the realm of the phenomenal. As we all know, the universe rewards action, so once again, congratulations for taking that first step. So, where do we go next?

Choice

How many of us have taken all the choice out of Relationships? Are you guilty of having said any of the following?

I had no choice.
He/She made me do it.
We had little choice but to do this.
Do you think I really wanted this to happen? There was no other way.

What if I suggest to you that nothing in relationships just happens? We all have choice. Choice to go with the flow, fight what isn't working or choose to create something more, something greater.

What if you had a totally different way, a new set of keys that opened up avenues of choice for you in every relationship? Wouldn't you then be interested in taking a step towards creating something greater with every relationship?

In this chapter, I'm going to be asking you questions. Why? Because a question opens up windows and doors to greater possibilities. A question gives you the space to receive the kind of relationship you've been asking for - joyous, nurturing, sensual, intimate and rewarding. A question empowers you to know what you know and acknowledge what works for you. You see, what creates a phenomenal relationship is one that works for you. For any relationship to work for you, you have to look at what is possible with somebody or something else and not give up on you. You have to be willing to be in the question of your life and your relationship.

So what would work for you?

Really...I'm asking you. What would work for you? Grab a journal and jot down your answer. As you begin to ask yourself more questions, each step on this journey becomes easier and you just may discover the ease of creating a thriving relationship, one that works for you and everybody else. Sound too easy?

> **What if a phenomenal relationship was an addition to your life and not a substitute?**

In working with the questions and tools I'm about to share with you, you will begin to uncover what works for you through your experiences. These tools will assist you in not only turning a good relationship into something greater but also tools that you can use when those challenging times appear in your life.

Warning: I will continue to ask you to carve out a space for you in working with me, so get a journal or a notepad and keep it with you. Treasure it and honor it.

As you ask these questions and work with your answers, you may have an awareness, a success, or simply the desire to step back a few paces. Whatever your awareness, write it down and ask...What else is possible?

It's a question I ask when things are great so more shows up and when things are really crappy so something far greater can show up.

So, let me ask you another question. What is a relationship for you? What does it look like for you? I would like you now to take a few minutes here just for you. This is what I like to call home play.

Get that pad and pencil and jot down your response, then write this down at the bottom:

What would it take to change this?

What else is possible?

Remember, the Universe is listening and its job is to respond to every question that you have. Would you be willing to let the universe go to work for you?

What would it take for you to be in total loving allowance of you in every relationship?

Judgement

How much have you been taught to judge yourself? I can remember the moment I learned to judge myself. It was back when I was about ten years old, having a great time at sleep away camp, dancing with my friends. We were having an absolute blast, laughing with the joy of being alive when a boy I knew from home came up to me and said, "Why are you such a show off."

Notice there is no question there. Can you feel the density of judgement? How much do we choose to allow those comments to form who we are, what we are and how we are? Discernment and judgement are conclusions. They hold you in place. There is no room for choice, question or possibility.

As long as you are doing judgement you are creating a conclusion so something that doesn't match that conclusion can never show up. The consequence of trying to create you to fit into someone else's idea of a relationship is that you then begin to separate and disconnect from your true self, from true choices and from consciousness.

What most of us are looking for, and rarely see, is a conscious relationship: one that radiates communion and oneness. In oneness, everything exists and nothing is judged. And really, isn't that more of what you're really looking for?

So what happens is, we get into a relationship and then we start to judge. I read an article once about a man and woman who were dating. One day the woman sits the guy down and says, "Let's have an argument." The guy raises his eyebrow and says, "No, that doesn't work for me." The woman says, "But it's really exciting! Arguing gets

15

the adrenaline going! And then we can have great makeup sex!"

The man declines. The next day, he gets a letter from her that says, "I don't think we have anything in common. We can't go out again."

Wow!

How many people depend on judgement to create excitation and then get turned on by the adrenaline rush and call that great sex? What would it take to generate being present beyond this reality? What would that look like?

That's why we're here. We ask questions on how to go beyond. For me it's always about being in the question. Who am I being when I'm judging me? I'm not being me.

What if you didn't have a me that you could define or confine? What if you were everything? What if you could be everything you wanted to be? If that were the case, if someone requires something of you, you can be that for them, without giving up any of you.

Your Reference Points

Do your reference points work for you? Well, when people refer to reference points they are usually referring to their experiences of their life in the past. It's almost like they trap themselves with what happened in the past as the only possible future outcome. There is no invitation there, no question, no choice.

Are reference points ever based on the present situation? Not the way this reality teaches us to use them. They are always limited, and based on past experience. In using them you distract yourself from the present because you are using the past to create a result.

I can hear you saying, "But how do you function without reference points?" The way to lose your reference points is to ask, "who does this belong to," or "who am I being here?"

When you start asking questions like these or even...

"Who else am I being?

"What else is possible?

You are inviting possibility into your life and expanding your focus and perception to what the world and universe can actually gift you. You're not creating something that's not there, you're just letting go of something that's not working for you. It's up to you. It's your choice. You have to be willing to be present. Now make a demand for something greater to show up. Know that the universe has your back in every choice you make, in every relationship.

> **Choice creates awareness. Awareness creates possibilities.**

As long as you're willing to be present, to make a demand, choice becomes who you become and you will never get caught again in a relationship that doesn't work for you and you will begin to create nurturing, joyous, phenomenal relationships with you and everyone you choose.

Choice and question go hand in hand. Questions create choice, which creates more contribution to you, which creates more. It's all in the creation of you. Anything that doesn't allow that, destroy it, let it go.

Susan Lazar Hart transforms the way people experience relationships and intimacy. As the Executive Creator of Right Relationship for You™ (RRFY), she travels the world offering Right Relationship™ classes and training her global network of RRFY™ Facilitators. With her straightforward approach and her irreverent sense of humor, Susan combines the tools of Access Consciousness™ with her experience as a wife, mother, artist, life coach and relationship counselor to inspire people around the world to search for new realities in every relationship. Susan holds a CFMW from Access Consciousness, a Professional and Personal Coaching Certification from Concordia University, as well as a Masters in Fine Arts Degree. www.susanlazarhart.com.

Chapter 4

Live Your Own Life and Never Get Lost Again

Dorinda Gay

"Beyond a doubt, if we sit in stillness long enough each day to hear the rhythm of Earth and Sky deep in our own bodies, we will find ourselves and never get lost again."

Love Always, The Universe

That one phrase, recently Guided to me, neatly summed up my thirteen-year journey from a professional trumpet player in New York City to an energy intuitive living in the Hudson Valley. What a ride! Yet so worth it.

There are infinite ways to 'find yourself.' Who we are is a reflection of where we reside. It is imperative to create life's most essential ingredient, Sacred Space, in the places where we spend our time; home and office. Within Sacred Space, innately your rhythm is felt strong and clear. It directs you every day to the place that your truth deeply resounds and is aligned with Earth, Sky and All That Is. Living from that inner knowing, rather than reacting to external voices, creates harmony within.

During my crazy ride from 2002 to now, I learned how to create strong energetic foundations by clearing and attuning space. Spaces where you can think, feel and act upon your own intuitive sense, not someone else's. My passion on Earth was born.

Exactly how did I evolve from professional musician to an energy intuitive clearing spaces?

After spending a few years reading 'woo-woo' new-age books, it became clear that music was no longer my professional calling. The innate beauty of playing was overshadowed by the 'inner workings of the business.' Though an active freelancer and teacher, my heart was calling me elsewhere. Then pivotal events occurred in my life. In 1997 my brother unexpectedly passed, and on Sept 11, 2001, I watched the events unfold across the river from my Astoria, Queens home. It became abundantly clear my world was changing.

I just knew there was more to life than I could see. One day, like a movie scene, I walked along the streets of Manhattan. I looked towards the sky and said, "So? What? What do you want me to do?!?"

Be ready to receive what you ask for. In 2002 my formal space clearing training with the Universe began something like this:

Universe: Dorinda, Go to St Louis, Missouri. Take an introductory class to become an intuitive spiritual counselor.

So, I did. And later I discovered this class was held in the same hotel where my spouse attended her high school prom.

Universe: Okay, Dorinda. The first class is complete. You discovered, "Hey! This stuff feels really, really familiar!" Now go to rural Missouri and take a 5-day class.

So, I did.

Universe: OK, now that you are here, your strong sense of direction will no longer serve you. You'll get lost driving, find yourself on deserted backroads, encounter road blocks, 'random' traffic accidents and meet people caught between worlds, who need help crossing to the other side.

WHAT?!? The other side? Between Worlds? Yup, that happened for a whole week. It's a miracle I attended the class at all. The Universe provided this extracurricular learning experience. Insane, right?? Yet within my own voice, it felt totally 'real' and 'natural'. I was waking up.

Long story short: Spirits started showing up in the middle of the night. They wanted help. I said "No, No, NO! I Am Not Living This Way." I don't know what YOU (Universe) want me to do, but it will not be this! And for goodness sake, wayward spirits, have the decency to show up with your whole body! Partial bodies are unnerving.

My life changed. Suddenly I could sense and see spirits. They couldn't see me. The Universe and I made an agreement. If I could help cross a soul or sweep a space, they would simply ask. It's my passion! Why? It lightens the energetic load on our beautiful planet. It creates more good vibes and light for all of us. My insatiable need to vitally engage human life is a part of me too! I simply couldn't have lost souls interrupting my play time.

I discovered a new word: Boundaries. Within them, I learned how to live a normal life as an intuitive. Sort of.

Universe: Okay Dorinda! Now that you have expressed free will in what you want, we are going to show you how to clear spaces. You will learn how to read the energy imprints of a building. How to look at the land and see history or echoes hanging around. This accumulated residue, when built up, stops the flow of vital life force for those residing in that space.

Uhhhh. Really?!?

Universe: Your first call for space clearing an actual house will be in....Wait for it....INDIA.

WHAT?!? Are you kidding me? India?

Universe: What's the worst that can happen?

Well...I could make a total fool of myself while surfing these crazy wild brained fantasies that I actually see and feel energy. I could lose connection to my neatly packaged sense of reality as I know it. No Biggie.

Universe: Heh. Do it Anyway.

How it Went:

Hello? Hello, this is Dorinda. We had an appointment so I could clear your house (In freakin India!)

I start seeing pictures in my head. I share what I see. The person on other end of the phone says: "That's exactly what I am looking at." I start to hyperventilate. The walls of my present existence come tumbling down. I reach for a brown paper bag, breathe and calmly say....

Okay, excellent. Then we are on the right page. (as if I've done this for years!)

So it goes. Spirit snickers in the background. Light dawns on marble head and blows my inner knowing wide open. There is no going back. Knowledge I already possess is being revealed to me here and now. This is my new life, complete with different rules and a new reality. No biggie.

Fast forward from 2003 to now.

What I have learned and how does this help you?

We are energy beings, learning, living and loving on this planet in physical bodies. With that comes a sensitivity and awareness of the life beating deep within our bodies, minds and spirits. Yet, we are surrounded by intense external distractions that pull us away from that Knowing. Without proper nourishment of space within, the outward influences can overtake and disconnect us from ourselves. Accessing this stillness (sanity!) is vital so we can hear, feel and act upon our inner voices. We can live a life that feels whole, worthy and blessed.

Skeptics and believers alike, call this "New Age." I'm a very big skeptic. I say, "It's not New Age. It's Energy, Life-Force!" It's the very thing that runs through your body, connecting you to You. It has nothing to do with purpose, destiny or fate. It has everything to do with feeling good.

Society defines success by the size of your house or car you drive. Lasting success is much different. It comes from living in alignment with your rhythm, while experiencing energy exchanges from others and our spectacular Mother, Earth. These exchanges are not about money, they are about LOVE.

Have you ever walked into a room and just knew there had been dissonance between people without a word being spoken? Ever feel moved by standing beside the ocean, in the mountains or sitting beneath a tree? Heard of an EKG? It measures the energy of your heart and how it beats in your body.

Have you had the desire to put your finger in a light socket to see what happens? Or stand outside holding a metal staff in a lightning storm? No you don't and even though your Mother told you not to, You already know this. As a natural conductor of energy, your intuitive body immediately let you know that putting your finger in a light socket creates discord. It isn't pleasant. Life is about creating harmony around you, not dissonance.

Doesn't it feel great at the end of the day to change your clothes or get into a bed with clean sheets? You are tired from your day and all of its external distraction. (This includes TV, computers and mobile devices!) All the outside energy has collected in your clothing and energy field. Your space within knows you are releasing and exchanging the accumulated energy in your clothing for clearer, new energy.

Let's apply this principle to your environment. Just as your knowing resonates and extends beyond your physical sense, so does your living and working space. When your body, mind and spirit are in harmony with your surroundings, you feel vibrant, grounded, connected and safe. There is energetic room to think, feel and act upon your Inner Voice, rather than living by external influence. You create the place to access Sacred Stillness which is vital to your Sanity.

Living or working in a space with energy 'build-up,' like worn clothing, or day to day stresses, creates dissonance. You may feel lethargic, disconnected, out of sorts. Or even depressed. You take the garbage out and shower regularly, right? You wouldn't wear the same clothing five days in a row, so why live or work in a space that blocks your own vitality and ability to experience life fully?

The number one rule to knowing if your space is aligned with you: If something doesn't feel right, it probably isn't! Trust your intuitive sense!

How do you fix something that 'just doesn't feel right' in your space? Two words: Beauty and function.

Everyone has "stuff." Does the stuff around you support or block the natural flow and rhythm within your space? Surrounding yourself with stuff that is beautiful and functional to you, is the key to lasting success. It creates Space Within, Stillness (Sanity) and creative flow.

Too much stuff blocks both Life-Force and your inner voice. It creates "energetic noise'" and external distraction that quiets your voice. In that space you feel neither good, or aligned.

Like dirty clothing, unused stuff collects energy debris if not loved (beautiful) or used (functional). Excessive stuff stagnates flow and makes you feel yucky. Over time, it can even lead to illness. For space to feel good and energetically aligned, surround yourself with stuff that you love and use.

Re-Aligning Your Space

1. Admit to yourself the areas of your space that 'just don't feel right.'

2. One by one determine if each item in this space brings beauty or function.

3. Do not organize yet! Simply remove and donate or release (trash) stuff that is not beautiful or functional.

4. Re-arrange your space with the beautiful and functional items that remain.

Note: Things you love or cherish bring beauty. It's okay to keep some of them.

Keep in Mind: Do small bursts in small spaces! Even 15 or 30 minutes at a time, unless you are really feeling good in flow. The biggest error is 'taking on too much' and feeling overloaded. The need to reconnect with Sacred Stillness (Sanity) is imperative.

Too simple to make a profound difference you say? Just try it. Remember: You are an energy being. You innately know not to put your finger in a light socket.

> **You have done the above, and it still doesn't 'feel right.'**

Energy, though rarely seen, is always felt! Old echoes in your space and the land are inherently present. They can accumulate overtime. The stresses may occur daily or be residue from past traumas, (yours or others), the property's history or even earthbound spirits. Trust your gut. These unsettled feelings are real!

Contacting a professional to clear and heal your space while attuning it to your innate rhythm creates harmony for everyone, including pets! A solid foundation to access Stillness is set. Within it Love resides. Within your Sacred Space you will find yourself and never feel lost again.

Dorinda Gay, founder of From The Universe To You, Inc., describes herself as an energy intuitive whose inner voice, along with Spirit's, guides her clearly to

24

live and love deeply on this planet. She maintains an active private practice in Croton on Hudson, NY and serves as an energy and space clearing consultant to homes and businesses across the country. She is building an Energy Teaching program to assist others in bringing forth their own healing gifts. Exploring the mysterious wonder of Earth drives her to lead journeys in magical Sedona. She considers joy, connection and play vital to living well. DorindaGay.com, Fromthe-universetoyou.com.

Chapter 5

In The Stillness...I Am Enough

Lisa Crofton, RMT

It was an unusually warm Saturday in April of 2008...my latest 3-day consulting contract had been postponed and I was grateful. My schedule had been maddening as of late and the break was welcomed. I was exhausted mentally and physically from pushing too hard in all areas of my life so when I awakened that April day to unusual New England warmth, I suggested my family and I take the hour drive to the shore to one of our favorite waterside restaurants for lunch. They were luke-warm on the idea but I cajoled so we piled into the car and headed to the shore.

Being sensitive is both a blessing and a curse when your awareness is at half mast. Despite my own excitement about going I was picking up on each of my family members' different states of unrest; my husband's increasing agitation over the traffic, the fact we were using up most of his chore day and the money we were spending (a favorite, frequent fear), my daughter's worry she would be cold by the water (she'd forgotten a jacket), and my son's complaint about forgetting his sunglasses. All this moaning adding to my growing angst. I was trying desperately to block out this negative energy as I focused on the beautiful passing scenery. My lame cheerful attempts to boost everyone's mood only acted as a temporary band-aid.

We arrived at the restaurant as a family in disarray; the breeze convinced my daughter she would indeed be cold (I handed her my jacket), my son complained about the sun in his eyes, (we selected a tented table), then my husband realized the restaurant only took cash, (we didn't bring any); luckily there was an ATM on premises. We finally settled at our table, but things did not really settle down. My husband, already in an agitated state, could not seem to pull himself out; his sarcasm continued and I continued to take it on energetically. At a certain point as I tried desperately to fight the blackness that was consuming me I began to feel nauseous and then I literally felt a buzzing in my head followed by awful dizziness…I put my hand to my head and said, "I feel a little dizzy" and then… NOTHING.

I have no recollection from that moment on until I woke up hearing my name being called and…a feeling of peace…I felt peaceful.… yet a little bothered at being woken up. Why were people disturbing my sleep? And why did they look so frantic? Then it began to sink in…I was laying on the deck of the restaurant looking up at the blue sky. My focus was returning…what happened to me? I could see my husband standing close to me, my daughter in panicked 'take charge' mode and my 16 year old son standing outside this onlooker crowd looking terrified. Even through my blurry vision that image will always remain crystal clear. A stranger was holding my head in her hands; apparently a nurse having lunch at a nearby table. I appeared to have had a seizure. An ambulance was called and I was taken to a nearby emergency center.

It's funny what you remember…as I lay in this public place with many onlookers I realized that I was lying in a puddle of liquid. I recalled our drinks being delivered just before getting dizzy…I knew in that moment there was only one of two reasons I could be soaking wet; one affected my dignity…my eyes scanned the table to count the drinks on the table: all four drinks were still in place on the table. Damn. Funny what we remember…today I think of that particular recall as the first divine sign reminding me that control is an illusion.

Following the emergency center visit I underwent two weeks of thorough testing – the results came through an EEG…a test used to evaluate the electrical activity in the brain. The determination: I suffered a Grand Mal Seizure; a type of generalized seizure that involves both sides of the brain. Many times people who have a Grand Mal will never have another, but most times Grand Mal Seizures are caused by Epilepsy…my diagnosis: 'late onset epilepsy', a diagnosis I did not take with style or grace and was completely unprepared to hear.

On the morning I was to receive the test results, I was scheduled to teach a workshop all day across the street from the doctor's office. I scheduled the doctor's appointment for first thing so I could just run straight to class after getting cleared…ever the multi-tasker and that day would be no different. In fact, I was suffering from a very bad respiratory infection with laryngitis so I was meeting another instructor just before class to receive throat lozenge's she swore would get me through class. I was certain my doctor would simply be admonishing me for the level of stress I was under, pointing out that a Grand Mal Seizure was a wake-up call, order me to slow down and then she would give me something for my respiratory infection and I would head to class. I had every angle covered…I was always in control.

Instead, I was greeted very gently and everyone seemed to be waiting for me when I arrived at the doctor's office. It was very off-putting. Still my ego was firmly in control and we were in Defcon 5 so I worked hard to maintain control. She spoke…I resisted.

As she calmly and gently revealed the results of the test, I defensively suggested it must be a mistake and I demanded to see the results she was holding in her hand. Even as I was speaking, I knew I sounded ridiculous. I felt desperate and angry as she was assuring me this condition could be controlled by a daily medication I would need to stay on for the rest of my life. Rest of my life? This could happen again? She went on to say that they had already taken the liberty of setting an appointment for me for the next day with a neurologist. A what? My next question: How long will this take? I have to teach in 10 minutes. Can I just have something for this infection? Her response: "Lisa, you are not teaching today and yes, I will give you something for your infection." As I stood there listening to them schedule my neurologist appointment, the real struggle in my brain began; I didn't know it yet but everything changed for me that day. I was about to learn that when we won't give up control the universe takes charge.

The first weeks and months after my diagnosis were the most difficult of my life. The part of my brain affected by the seizure was the front left temporal lobe; the part of the brain that controls language, memory and the ability to use words. Really? Was this a great cosmic joke? As a writer, teacher, coach and lecturer I could not have been more devastated…or scared. I was immediately put on an anti-seizure medication which was meant to 'slow me down'; if the seizure didn't kill me, this should. Per state law, my driver's license was taken away for three months. I was driven to and from everywhere; my loss of independence was humbling. What was worse…and terrifying…for the first time in my life I was unable to retrieve words, sometimes the words that actually came out of my mouth were incomprehensible (a side effect of the medication), my short and long term memories had suffered damage and my greatest perceived skill, communication, was severely handicapped.

My newspaper column came to a screeching halt, my 8-year greeting card writing contract fizzled and my dream of becoming a best-selling author died with my language skills. Without the ability to go 180 miles an hour with my hair on fire I simply did not know who I was and neither did those around me. I simply wasn't emotionally available in a familiar way. My husband, children and friends had always been able to come to me with any issue but now I was in the spiritual, mental and physical fight of my life. What was happening?

Okay, I got this…I thought. At first I simply handled it the way I did everything else in my life, in control, as though nothing had changed; in stubborn denial trying to put all the pieces back together. THAT was NOT working…physically my brain had changed, my stamina was severely hindered and I could not fight the descending feeling of discouragement. Debilitating fear would rise up in my throat each time the realization would hit me that my future and my dreams, as I had attached myself to them, were no longer viable. Writers need the ability to retrieve words, speakers need to think easily on their feet and authors need their memories. I struggled with all three; I did not know who I was without the ability to express myself through the eloquent and persuasive use of language.

As time wore on my grief deepened; slowly I felt myself become more anxious and depressed. Being intimately familiar with grief, having gone through the process many times before it finally became abundantly clear to me that it was my own life 'before' the seizure I needed to both mourn and release. If I was going to heal myself emotionally and learn to live a full life again I would need to allow the coveted dreams of who I was to 'die' and allow a new me to be 'reborn.' It required letting go of the way I, 'wanted things to be' and embracing them the way, 'they actually were'. This began the long steady process of healing and finally getting aligned with my soul.

As spiritual pioneers we often hear the words, "spiritual align-ment" and we may intellectually know what those words mean; to live a heart based life while following our soul path. In my personal experience even knowing the truth of the words didn't mean I was paying attention to them. Prior to my brain literally seizing up, I pushed many things down when I heard the little voice whisper to me: 'this person isn't good for you', 'you do not agree with this work', 'this place is not healthy for you', 'those opinions are not yours.' But I did not listen because I was afraid that to resist was to be rejected, to challenge might cause loss, and disagreement would bring about separation. I became what others expected and in the process became an image of those expectations. It was how I knew others loved me and it became how I loved myself. And it was slowly killing me. My heart was being ignored and my inner sadness grew…but I could not see it…I was too busy living up to expectations and believing the ultimate lie…I was not enough.

Surrendering to the reality of my situation is how my awareness began to bring meaning to the experience. Once I gained clarity I re-alized that I needed to search deeper within to discover my authentic-ity instead of attaching myself to the image of what I thought made me ME. In the stillness, I found something astonishing; I found the quiet guiding voice that knew all my truths. Through quiet meditation and mindfulness I slowly found my heart, and the gentle, loving being that was always there. Opening my heart led to guidance that showed me how my healing and spiritual lifestyle would benefit many. Today I love myself in unconditional, nurturing ways that allow me to care for myself and show others how to do the same. I use this self-penned mantra as a reminder that, 'I am enough' without expectation or perfection.

Just Be, Just Love, Love Me, Be Me, Be Love. ©2013
I hope you will use it too. The small still voice always knows.

Lisa Crofton is a Spiritual Intuitive, Life Mastery Coach and Soul Re-alignment Practitioner as well as a Reiki Master Teacher. She is co-founder of the Bloom Life Mastery Coach Training School in Southington, CT and runs Lotus Moon Studios, LLC, a holistic healing center. Lisa offers unique Intuitive Life Mastery Coaching for private clients and groups as well as online teaching programs and retreats. Combining 30 years of entrepreneurial experience, holistic healing training certifications and tapping into her own intuitive methods, Lisa guides others to discover their soul's blueprint and follow the unique path that lights their life on fire! www.lotusmoonstudios.com, lotusmoonreiki@gmail.com.

Chapter 6

Enhance Your Psychic Ability and Make Your Life Magical

Anna Clayton, MA

You have psychic ability, whether you know it or not! You also have the ability to heal yourself, to manifest what you need, and to allow magic to flow through your life. I'm living proof - I was an atheist for the first 20 years of my life, and now I'm a psychic healer.

I was raised without religion, in fact, my father mocked people who believed in God. But I was always a seeker of truth. My mother died when I was 20, confronting me with difficult questions about the meaning of life, and I realized that although I was studying philosophy, it was not a comfort to me in my grief. I consciously took a leap of faith.

After my mother's death, my stepfather gave me Shirley MacLaine's book, "Out on a Limb." Her straightforward account of how she turned into a spiritual person through her own direct experience changed my life. I decided to open my mind, and only believe in things that I had experienced myself. I began to explore spirituality.

Psychic Ability Gets Stronger the More You Use It

I learned that we all have psychic ability, but we are just taught to ignore it. It's like a muscle that strengthens the more you practice. As I have always been able to feel the feelings of others, I already had the psychic ability of sensing (clairsentience), so I decided to test myself to develop my clairvoyance (psychic sight). I started by reaching into my sock drawer and guessing what color sock I was holding. It was random at first, but the more I did it, the more accurate I got. Those were the days before caller ID or cellphones, so when the phone rang, I would try to guess who was calling me. Again, I rapidly became very accurate, and then, when I found myself thinking of friends, they would call me or I'd run into them.

I realized that we are all connected. I believe we are all the Divine (God) just playing at being separate from itself, so that it can have every experience - because if you were omnipotent and omnipresent, you'd get bored too! So we are literally all one consciousness. Because of that, psychic ability is natural: we are all tuned into each other, we just need to become aware of it.

Be The Hero of Your Own Story

The Divine offers guidance if you start to pay attention. Jung talked about synchronicity or "meaningful coincidence." Louise Hay talks about the symbolism of illness and injury to specific body parts, and what the lesson is that needs to be learned. A common saying is, "there are no accidents."

I found that the more you allow yourself to notice the magic in the world, the more Divine Grace will come through and guide you. I experimented with the thought, "If my life were a book or a movie, what is the theme, what is the symbolism?" A whole new level of meaning opened up to me because I was willing to see it.

The World is a Mirror

I realized that I had been living with blinders on - I had not had eyes to see the magic that was all around me. When I became open to what the Divine was trying to tell me, I started having psychic experiences and seeing "coincidences" all the time - the Divine happily partnered with my quest for meaning.

I realized that since we are the Divine pretending to be separate from itself, the purpose of life is to learn to be yourself, and also to realize that the existence of a separate self (our ego) is actually an illusion. That's the cosmic joke. The world is set up as a mirror, to show us how we are actually creating our lives through what we focus on - as the saying goes, "energy flows where attention goes." The Buddha said, "Our thoughts are things. With our thoughts we make the world." God loves you so much that whatever you focus on gets supported - whether positive or negative.

That can sound daunting until you realize that it means you are completely responsible for your life, which is a good thing. If you heal the conflict in yourself and get clear on what you want, you can heal yourself and even the world around you. The more you heal and release, the more Divine Grace has the space to come in and shape your life. The more you look for spiritual lessons, the more they will be revealed.

How to Heal the Conflict Within

In order to manifest what you want, you need to stop manifesting what you don't want. Here's a psychology technique that you can use when you wonder why you aren't getting what you think you want.

The first step is to realize that although your conscious mind may want something, if your life isn't working, it probably means there are unconscious parts of you who want something different.

It is normal for all of us to have different parts to our personality, (although we only hear about it with people who are so traumatized they get stuck in different personalities at different times.) When you say things like, "I'm not myself today," that reflects awareness that there is more than one self!

Here's a healing exercise for working with the different parts of you.

1) Relax and close your eyes.
2) Imagine that you are in a theater by yourself, looking at an empty stage.
3) Invite a personality part to come and speak to you. If you know you are having a particular issue or block, you can request that part to come forward, for example: "I am inviting any part of me that is afraid of change to come and speak to me." Or just invite part of you to come to the stage and find out who they are.

4) Give it a minute or two.

5) Just allow yourself to start to see an image on the stage.

6) Does it have a shape? A color? Is it a human? A monster? An animal?

7) Interview it about its feelings in a compassionate way, talk to it like you would talk to a friend in distress.

8) Realize that every part of you, no matter how dysfunctional, thinks it is helping you. With practice, you can figure out why it is doing what it is doing (or not doing).

9) Reason with it and speak kindly to it. Example: "I understand you are afraid of change. I know change can feel scary, but I need to leave this career and find one that will make me happy and I need your support."

10) Give it a new job! Example: "You've done a great job of avoiding change, but now I want to give you a new job, is that okay? Please help me to be flexible about changing and help me to create the support I need to change!"

11) Thank it, let it go.

12) Repeat the process as often as necessary.

The more you practice that technique, the more you will get out of your own way and be able to access your inner guidance.

How to Ask for What You Want

Part of living a magical life is manifesting what you need. Prayer works if you pray sincerely, then let it go and trust that God will provide. Gratitude is a form of prayer and a way of saying, "more of this, please!" Here's the best way that I have found to manifest.

I have found that when manifesting, it is more important to focus on the feeling of gratitude and the right words, than to visualize, although if you are a visual person you can do that too. I had to teach myself how to pray since it wasn't something I had grown up doing. The best way that I have found is this:

1) Clear your mind.

2) Get grounded.

3) Find the right words (no negatives, find a way to express it in the positive).
4) Drop into your heart, into that place of quiet knowing.
5) Feel deep gratitude as if it has already happened.
6) From that place, pray for what you want. You can even pray as if it has already happened but that is not required.
7) Let it go. Realize that it is in God's hands.
8) Have faith that your prayer will be answered.

Awakening to the Truth Within

Awakening (enlightenment) is possible, in fact, it is our life purpose. We are all on the path to Awakening. I awakened in 2007 after studying with various awakened teachers for a number of years. Awakening means losing the sense of being a separate self, and awakening to the Truth of the Divine within us all.

Awakening is healing in itself, because it causes the identification with ego, the small self, to fall away, and bring in inner peace. The ego is what causes suffering. Identification with ego is at the root of addiction. In a sense, everyone is addicted to something, whether it is attention, drama, suffering, feeling sorry for yourself, putting others first to the point of losing your own identity, shopping, eating unhealthy food - the list is endless. All of these attachments and cravings take us out of ourselves and keep us from feeling our feelings. If we don't let ourselves feel our feelings, we stay stuck in them and they don't heal.

In order to heal, we have to have to courage to truly face ourselves. The more you can be honest with yourself, the less you will suffer, even if the honesty entails allowing yourself to feel anger, grief, or fear. Those feelings can only heal if we allow them to come up and out, without judging the feelings or trying to fix them.

Don't Believe Your Own Stories

You are so much more than you think you are. You are more than a brain or a body, more than your feelings, more than the roles you have taken on. You are a magical, multi-dimensional, immortal soul.

The more you can step back and view yourself from the position of a compassionate observer (the Buddhist idea of non-attachment); the more space you give yourself to change, and the more you allow Divine Grace into your life. There are many Awake teachers on the planet at this time, so seek out their writings and teachings if you feel guided to do that. The more you can expose yourself to awakened people and their teachings; through reading, meditating, attending lectures; the more you will raise your own vibration and ripen your energy system for Awakening.

Awakening is possible, and it is your destiny. I started studying energy healing in 2004. In 2012, while in a meditation, my spiritual teacher appeared to me and gave me a download of energy that I thought was a healing for me, but I was told that it was my own healing gift, Mother's Milk Divine Mother Energy. I was told to go back to that place in Consciousness to request many additional downloads of the healing tools.

With these gifts, I am able to clear issues at the karmic level, and I help my clients connect to their own inner wisdom and release whatever is blocking them from living from that place of Truth. I do not work with guides, I am able to access and channel the Divine directly so that people are reconnected to and healed by the Source. I am able to work through Divine Consciousness to go below the level of ordinary consciousness and clear issues at the root, by-passing resistance that sometimes arises. In this way I can awaken the issue itself and release it rather than just making you feel better. I have been blessed to Awaken one client so far and to help prepare others for their eventual Awakening.

Healing is magic and transformation is possible. You have the ability to access Divine Grace within, to heal, access the Truth, and manifest the life you really want. Allow Divine Grace into your life and see what happens!

Anna Clayton, MA, LMFT, is an Intuitive Healer with her own unique healing gift, Mother's Milk Divine Mother Energy. She is also a licensed psychotherapist, a certified herbalist and shamanic healer, and a certified holistic health and nutrition coach. She combines this expertise with her psychic healing abilities to create Transformational Healing. She is able to clear issues below the level of consciousness, at the karmic level and even the genetic level. She offers individual sessions in person and at a distance. To contact Anna or to book a session, please see her website, http://www.InsightfulTransformation.com.

Chapter 7

The Golden Thread of Oneness

Barbra Richards, AC

At the ripe old age of two or three, I remember my Grandmother saying, "Barbra, look. Isn't this beautiful?" I looked up from play to find a flower as big as my head held out in front of me as I was invited to inhale its sweet perfume. I didn't have words for those feelings at the time, but I felt such a fascination and wonder. And now, looking back, I can say something deep within me stirred and I knew it was very important I pay attention.

On our trips away from Jersey City, she would point out the vastness of the ocean, cartoon characters in cloud formations, and month by month she would introduce me to the changing of the seasons and all the glorious facets of Nature. In each of these instances, her face reflected such an inner joy and tranquility of all that surrounded her as she watched me closely to see if I understood.

One day my Grandmother brought me into a room that I had never been in before. Cautiously, I peeked through the doorway and saw three huge cages filled with tiny birds chirping and hopping from perch to perch. I remember thinking: Why are they in cages? A part of me felt sad, but I didn't know why.

She then began to tell me their names and their relationship to each other, "This is Myrtle, and her brothers, Harry and Charles. This is their Mama and Papa. Baby Myrtle grew up, married Joe, and they moved into their own home over by the window," and so it went. And I thought: How perfect, but really?

It was then that all creatures caught my utmost fascination as I immediately recognized them as miniature beings, with miniature minds, miniature feelings, and miniature agendas, within their own miniature communities just like my Grandmother's birds. There was no doubt in my mind that they were the same as us, only smaller, and shared that One intangible Life Force common to all life.

When I was four, my mother brought me to live in her home with her boyfriend at the time, and my life changed immediately and drastically. Growing up through the chaos that raged around and at me, I quickly recognized the contrast of consolation and peace that the Animals and Nature offered me, especially my fascination with all the forms of life that made their way across my path. Nature and its inhabitants became my playground and my solace so much so I would seek them out. Slowly, through their reflection, I began to discover an inner awareness of who I was and how life was truly meant to feel. I would laugh with the squirrels as they played and scampered and dropped nuts on my head; and the birds who would give birth to baby birds in the spring and then fly south in the fall. All together in synchronized measure, trailed by a soaring imagination of me flying away with them.

My fur babies, mostly dogs that were brought home, made my connection even deeper as I could talk to them and they seemed to talk to me. I could hold them in my arms and hug them, and in their own way, they hugged back. They gave me a sense of community; a sense of family. To this child, they became my go-to beings, a nurturing, safe haven that sometimes I had to visit in secret to give and receive what we both so needed.

Rexi was my grammar school companion in all things; a little, brown, mixed-breed pound puppy whose nightly walks became one of my favorite "chores" long before my parents brought him to a farm for a better life. I still remember looking back at him as he kept trying to run towards the car as we drove away.

Rebel was my next animal companion who was picked up on the street, and for the most part of his life with us was confined to his bed, except on nights when my parents would go out. Within minutes of hearing the car drive away, I would entice him down the forbidden hallway into my room where he'd pounce onto my bed and burrow deep down under my covers and we would roll around and play together. Miraculously, he began to do it on his own! Shortly after the car would pull away, I would hear him dashing down the hall and I'd take cover. Shortly before he disappeared, he kept running away from home. I overheard my step-father say that he was spending time with a family on the next block and his attempts to catch him weren't very successful. I didn't quite understand why when I found him, he turned, looked back at me, and after a long hesitation, he ran further away. I knew in my heart it had nothing to do with me, but he knew it was time to move on for his own safety. I so hope he found a happier place.

Then there was King, a beautiful Shepherd/Collie mix with the gentlest spirit you could ever meet. It was Christmas when he arrived. He was a puppy and I was 17. Little did I know that eight years later I would be spending the last night of his life feeding him ice cubes, and waiting for the sun to come up so we could go to the vet. It was with a heavy heart a few days later that I walked outside on the way to my car and turned and looked wistfully at his empty dog house. I watched in amazement as he stepped out of it and walked the seven-foot or so distance from his house to the gate where I was standing, just like he always did every morning. I remember thinking, this has to be real because my eyes are following his movements! He looked like he had a smile on his face as he came right up to the gate, and then I saw him simply dissolve into the air. On my worst day, no matter how I willed to see him again, he never made himself visible. It was then I knew all life has a Spirit that lives beyond our senses.

These Keepers of my Heart came and went at home, and I knew that when someone new arrived, it would just be a matter of time before those beloveds would disappear as well and I, therefore, made them my all and gave them my all. I no longer swing and sing to the sun and sky as the days grow longer, nor lie in bed wondering what the crickets are saying as I listen intently through an open bedroom window.

This statement, once true when I wrote it, has now prompted many changes to my hectic life. Now when I look out my window I see an early morning fisherman wrangling with his fishing rod, or a swan gracefully sailing across the sky to her place on the lake. My lake house has brought it all back again, and there is an old wooden bench swing with peeling red paint where I sit and swing. I don't sing, but there's a constant reflection of peace and contentment and an inner smile that knows nothing touches the love and light reflected in the eyes of all animals and the peace and inspiration of Nature.

My Grandmother's greatest gift to me was awareness and how much MORE of Life there is to discover, regardless of one's immediate surroundings. It's a mystery and connection that needs expansion in many lives today, and I am certain this explains my sense of "coming home" when I discovered the Centers for Spiritual Living. Through their classes and teachings, I have also become a Licensed Interfaith Prayer Coach/Practitioner, and bring that into my Animal and Nature Ministry as well.

Now when I look into an Animal's eyes or surround myself in Nature, I am aware that the experience is much more than a lick on the nose, the purr of a kitten, or a seascape at sunset. It is a manifestation of the Golden Thread of Oneness mirroring its perfection and wholeness, through its own example of our true potential as we live and breathe amidst our human experience. I believe animals are sacred, authentic examples of the self-experiencing aspect of All that Is. Nature is their stage and animals are the stars of Its show. Intertwined, they dance an imprint of Love and Light into our souls.

This has been shown to me numerous times at an animal blessing when someone shares an issue they may be having with their animal companion, and after completing the session, I've looked up to find a visible reaction in the human as their furry companion brought to the surface something within themselves that needed healing.

Many smiles are born through tears of grief through conversation and memories of comical behaviors of transitioned animal companions who gently lead their humans to a deeper understanding of the gifts and lessons they teach us if only we are present and aware of the Golden Thread of Oneness.

As a facilitator of that awareness at end-of-life transitions, I take someone's hand and support them through their decisions, accompany them through the process of euthanasia, and afterwards offer a listening ear and a compassionate heart, memorial services and funerals.

Barbra Richards and her Animal and Nature Ministry, Paws, Prayers 'n People, was established after becoming an Animal Chaplain and a Credentialed Animal Bereavement Facilitator through the Emerson Theological Institute's Humane Division in 2012. Late Summer of 2015, she was licensed as a Spiritual Prayer Practitioner through the Connecticut Center for Spiritual Living. She provides services and celebrations for humans and their animal companions along the continuum of life. She lives in a small cottage overlooking a lake surrounded by nature and her three animal companions, Smudgy, Kismet and Charlotte, writing and offering inspiration and healing to humans and their animal companions. Contact Barbra at pawsprayersnpeople@gmail.com or www.pawsprayersnpeople.com.

Chapter 8

When Life Gives You Lemons...
Feng Shui Your Home

Shareane Baff

The supermarket is crowded with women with lifeless eyes walking swiftly to fill their cart with supplies to make dinner. Once in a while we give a small smile as we acknowledge one another. Most of us have worked all day, judging by our outfits and uncomfortable fitting shoes. We're fairly certain we're coming home to a chaotic, messy, maybe even dirty home. Will there be room on the counter or in the sink to start preparing dinner? Knowing my children, this is exactly what I will be coming home to. My soul and my body longs for peace, harmony, balance, joy and laughter and I believe my "sister shoppers" long for this too.

When I got married, my dream was to be at the table with my family at dinnertime and feed their soul as well as their body. I craved meaningful conversation. I wanted to encourage my children and give wise, wonderful, witty, pertinent advice. I wanted to listen, make eye contact and connect in a truly heart centered way. It was like that when they were little, but now my two daughters are teenagers and my younger daughter and my husband seem to be at each other most of the time. Now, dinner time is just something to get through with so you could go on with your life.

I had a good relationship with each daughter and my husband, but put us together and it was not the Walton family. It didn't match the picture of what I had envisioned for my life. My heart felt broken; in fact there was a huge hole where joy, sweetness, and peace should reside. I had a successful career, wonderful friends, a beautiful home, a nice car, five loving and loveable dogs, a HUNK of a husband, yet I was SAD, EMPTY, HOLLOW and in pain. How could this be? I tried to do everything right.

After all, I was SUPERWOMAN!

I knew there had to be a solution and I was going to find it. I talked to my Angels and guides as I have done since I was eight years old. I meditated, kept a journal, did daily gratitude exercises and I felt happier. The hole felt more defined and not so jagged but it was still there, the empty space was smaller.

SUPERWOMAN WAS NOT WHOLE!

So, what do I do when I am in crisis? I go to the library! It is there surrounded by volumes filled with wisdom, that I feel at home, grounded and connected. I know a book or two, or three, or four will fall off the shelf, leading me to the answers that I seek. I must become a sleuth and decipher the code. I'm good at this. I feel hopeful, confident and strong and I can feel my breath getting deeper. I will heal my heart! I will have peace in my soul, in my home, in my family. I grab a notebook and pens, and put on my winter coat and boots. It's cold outside but I feel warm and flushed. I'm a bloodhound. I know my answer will be there in the library.

I stand at the entrance to the library with the aisles of books before me. Now, do I go right, left or straight ahead? Still standing there looking for guidance, I ask my guides to give me the answer and point me in the right direction. I do this by dowsing, even using my purse as pendulum to get my answer. I usually get a clear signal, but this time I'm not getting anything. When I find a book I need, it's like my whole body lights up, but not this time. I feel good but I'm not being directed. I'm confused but I know that just like the Goddess Demeter, I will not give up. I find many books with inspirational words, but I'm still in search of the ones that will give me the answers I need. Leaving the library, I'm still hopeful. I know my Angels will guide me to where I need to go next.

The next morning, I receive a message when I am journaling. My guides tell me that I need to go to a bookstore in Manhattan and I will find what I need there, and am guided to look in the metaphysical section. I travel 100 miles to the bookstore in the city. When I get there I see that the metaphysical section is only a few shelves. As I stand there searching every row, and now lying on the floor, I finally find my prize there on the bottom shelf. Two books written by Sarah Rossback, Interior Design with Feng Shui and Feng Shui Design. JACKPOT! I have found what I need to heal my heart… but what is Feng Shui? I had heard of Feng Shui before but I had no idea what it really was or why it would work for me.

Feng Shui (pronounced Fung Shway) is a 5,000 year old Chinese art form of placement. We place furniture and objects in our home or office to create balance and harmony in our lives. Feng Shui unblocks the flow of Chi, the life force energy, for our home. No needles are necessary, but your clear and focused intention is a key component to success.

I'm an avid reader and so I quickly devour these two books, ready for more. Oh! There is no more. These are the only two books written in English. All the books written about Feng Shui are in Chinese, and I don't speak Chinese.

I'm confused. Why would my guides lead me to a dead end? As soon as I think this I hear laughter from my guides. They tell me, "You are never at a dead end. You have every answer you need in this life within you. It's for you to uncover, discover, create and manifest." They hold up a big sign that says…Meditate, Meditate, Meditate!

I was looking forward to a quick fix and I realize that I will have to devote time every day to meditate. My Angels have never let me down, and this time won't be any different.

This is not a superstition, as I thought when I started to study Feng Shui. It is not a religion; it is not smoke in mirrors, nor is it magic fairy wand, although it is magical. It is art, science and common sense combined. It allows for good design principles, nature, intuition and compassion to work together to balance your interior and exterior space. It is a powerful tool for transformation.

There are basic rules to follow in Feng Shui. You must approach Feng Shui with sincerity, an open heart and compassion. You must see with Feng Shui eyes. That means you see with eyes of compassion and love.

Reflect and dig deep…

    What is your inner truth?

    Respect your inner wisdom.

Listen to the small voice in your head, not the loud, commanding voice.

What do you want to change?

What do you need to change?

Set your intent...

Be ready to follow your intention with an action.

Reevaluate...

Life changes, and changes in you.

You must update your home and your Feng Shui adjustments.

Do not get stagnant, bored or boring.

Have fun...sing, dance, play, take a walk, and spend time with people you enjoy.

My daily meditations gave me insight into the Bagua (pronounced bog-wa), which originated from the I Ching. It's an eight sided map that you overlay on a floorplan. This floorplan can be your home, a room or a plot of land. Each of the eight sides and the center, represent a specific aspect of your life. You have the ability to transform any and all of these areas of your life.

* Health & Family
* Money & Abundance
* Fame & Reputation
* Love & Marriage
* Children & Creativity
* Helpful People & Blessings
* Career & Path in Life
* Spiritual Cultivation & Personal Growth

If you assess that you need to improve your health or the health of a family member, you will make adjustments in the center of the Bagua area. When I overlaid the Bagua over my home I concentrated on the areas of relationships, children and family. It was in these areas that I needed to make Feng Shui adjustments.

A very important part of Feng Shui is balancing the Five Elements: Wood...Fire...Metal...Water...Earth

All visible and invisible elements are in everything in our universe.

That means your physical, mental and spiritual energy is comprised of these elements in proportions that vary. You possess each of these elements in your own unique combination. However, there will be one element that is more dominant and defines you. You will also be Yin or Yang in that element.

This is such an important aspect of Feng Shui. When you walk into your home, your office, your friend's home, a restaurant or get in your car, you bring your element and the Yin and Yang of that element into the space. You change the balance and harmony of that space with your presence. When I looked at the issues in my home that I needed to change, it was the arguments, especially at dinnertime that upset me the most. I began to look at each of us and assess what element we brought to our home and dinner table.

I'm Yin Fire, my husband is Yang Fire. Fire people are emotional, passionate, enthusiastic, full of life, spontaneous and expressive. They wear their heart on their sleeve, lead with their heart and can forget to analyze a situation because their feelings overrule their head.

If you are Yang to that element, you may be argumentative, loud, and judgmental and lose your temper easily. You speed through life, conversations and dinners. You need to be on the move. If you are Yin to that element you will lose your spark, your joy and you will feel depleted and tired. You may want to be alone and you may become passive and fear the future. You can swallow your anger, not express yourself and internalize your feelings which can lead to internal illness. The organs in the body affected by an imbalance in fire are your small intestine and heart. So heart attacks, strokes, indigestion and acid reflux are indicative of this lack of balance.

My oldest daughter is Yang Earth. Earth people are the foundation that everything is built on. They are grounded, stable, reliable, caring and peacemakers. They are people that can be counted on. They say 'Yes' too often. When they are out of balance they often feel lethargic, without hope or have low self-esteem. They feel swallowed up, stuck or overwhelmed. They can sacrifice for others and not take care of themselves. The imbalance of earth energy can show up as cancer, depression and issues of the stomach or spleen.

My youngest daughter is Yang Wood. Wood people are kind-hearted and need to stay in their integrity and truth. They need

51

to grow. They will think and listen to all sides of an argument. They always try to be fair. They have long check lists and they often think too much. When they are balanced they make the best bosses. When a Yang Wood person is out of balance they will be very opinionated, judgmental and stop listening to others. Their voice and their opinions will be the only ones that matter. They are stubborn and will bully others into submission. When a Wood person is out of balance it can show up in the physical body as liver or gall bladder issues. In my home, three of the family members are yang, which means in order to balance my home I have to work with elements that will temper their energy. The element that tempers the Yang Fire is water. It can put out or dampen the fire. Water will also feed the wood so that it can grow. Adding the element of water might not be great for an earth person, as water and earth make mud, which means they will feel stuck.

I put the element of water in the house slowly, then wait to see the results. I use fountains and beautiful bowls of water with flowers floating in them. I use the color black, anything that is a free form shape, mirrors and objects that relate to water, such as turtles, frogs, and sea shells. I keep adding more water features to my home, setting my intention using Feng Shui chants. I wait a few days to a week and assess the progress.

It's like developing a recipe. Finally, I'm happy with the outcome and we can enjoy peaceful dinners together. We can live in balance, harmony and joy. I pat myself on the back. I feel whole and life is good!

BUT…All that water puts out my small Yin Fire. I'm not sad, I'm whole, but I have lost my spark, my creativity, my zest for life. I have lost the thing that makes me who I am. OKAY, it must be time to create another solution!

This time I concentrate on myself. What does Yin Fire need to keep the fire going? Wood of course, is the answer. I can't use too much wood because that would create an imbalance for my Yang Fire husband. I choose to use crystal to balance my energy. I use it to make myself bracelets using Green crystal because the color Green symbolizes wood energy. I make myself a 6 True Words bracelet that clears any negative energy from my space and brings in blessing.

I create a Five Elements bracelet to balance my energy and set my intention into the bracelet.

I become the Feng Shui.

Finally, I'm at peace. I feel balanced, whole and happy. Life is ever changing and will always bring us opportunities to grow. Often these opportunities will come as obstacles and hardships. There are always solutions, always!

When life gives you lemons, make lemonade!

Reflect, learn and practice Feng Shui or hire a professional. It will be well worth the cost. A balanced life is a necessity, not a luxury. Set your intentions, clear out your clutter and clear your home of unwanted energies. Never forget that LOVE is the most powerful force in the universe.

You are love and you are magic!

Shareane Baff has been a student of spirituality for what seems like her whole life. From as early as 8 years old, Shareane can remember hearing her angel's wisdom as she would pray for guidance. It was then that she developed an intimate relationship with the world of spirit. Shareane went on to graduate from the BTB Feng Shui Masters Training Program, and has had the privilege to study under Grand Master Lin Yun, among other master teachers and internationally recognized authorities on Feng Shui. Shareane is also the owner and creator of Intentions Jewelry. This unique collection combines Shareane's knowledge of Feng Shui and her trance mediumship skills allowing her to infuse the finest crystal with divine energy. Shareane works closely with and has developed a bracelet line for world renowned spiritual medium, James Van Praagh. Shareane is available for Soul to Soul consultations, Bracelet consultations, teaching and speaking engagements, and Feng Shui consultations. To learn more about Shareane visit www.intentionsjewelry.com.

Chapter 9

The Light Within

Tami Reagor, CHHC

Twinkling stars. Some shine brightly while others are dimmer. All stars have the same right to divinity within them, but some of us get lost along the way. In doing so our inner light dulls to where we can no longer hear, see or feel it. Underneath the surface it lies patiently waiting for you to reconnect to it, regardless of what you have or have not done in your life. I know you know what I am talking about – that inner hunger asking for recognition just below the surface. This hunger is your heart and soul yearning for you to discover who you really are and the reason why you chose to come here during this time.

What does your heart and soul yearn for? And what is standing in your way of achieving it?

To find these deep answers, you must reach down inside of yourself, which can be hard because it forces you to look at parts of your life that are not going the way you hoped. The parts of your life that aren't fulfilling, stir just below the surface with the heavy feelings of sadness, regret, resentment, anger and fear. These feelings can be overpowering, which makes it easier to stay stuck rather than face them to move forward.

The world we live in teaches us several things that makes looking at this harder. As children, our parents instill in us traditions and values that represent our culture and faith. Through this, many of us have been taught that it is selfish to focus on ourselves and that it is a sin to look within, for the answer is on the outside of yourself and only evil lies within.

Some may gasp, but being raised Roman Catholic taught me exactly that. As a child, I was taught that I did not have permission to find my own answers, they had to be right in God's eyes and the only way to do that was to ask the priest. If that wasn't limiting enough, I was taught that I could not ask for forgiveness for my sins without first divulging my shame and guilt to the priest, who then would authorize God's forgiveness in some form of penance. Now I understand through my own journey that this isn't true, the answers and forgiveness that I seek come from within when I connect to my inner light (soul). My soul then connects me to Source Energy (God).

As a Roman Catholic I was never taught that my soul was anything more than the piece that goes to heaven. But while that is one piece, your soul is so much more. It is your shining star – it represents the true you – it is what makes you tick and what makes you unique. It is your connection to Source Energy (God). Here you can gather the knowledge you need to live the life your soul desires.

We have been taught that in order to be successful and socially accepted we must fit in at all costs. This means being unique is not always looked at in a good light. By the time I was 10, I was almost 6 feet tall, and so I know all too well what it is like to not be like everyone else. I was made fun of relentlessly and all I wanted to do was make sure I blended in at all costs. Through all of this, I lost my compass to my inner light. I was never taught how valuable my inner light was and how much love and peace it can bring to life once you tap into it. Instead I joined the rat race – to live life like everyone else and fit in as best I could. But it never felt right, this hunger still teased me inside. Its need to be recognized continued to grow and I did all I could to figure out what it was trying to tell me. I took class after class all in the hopes of stumbling upon the missing link.

It has been a long journey but I have finally figured out what the missing link is and it turns out it was right in front of my face. What is it? It's within me – the answers lie within and through my intuition and my psychic sense of hearing, it talks to me.

As a divine being, you are meant to be YOU. Your inner light will show you the way to rediscover who you really are if you let it.

Do you trust your intuition to show you the path of least resistance to fulfilling your soul's desires?
Have you ever followed your intuition's guidance?
Has it ever lead you astray?

Your inner light knows the way for you to discover your soul's gift which is what makes you unique and is your gift to the world. The answers are within you – are you ready to find them?

What is coming up for you with this idea of going within to dig up your past hurts, mistakes and regrets? All these things are holding you back from discovering your soul's purpose. They weigh heavy on your soul and pull you away from your soul's journey. You can continue to let the world, family or friends tell you how to live your life or you can decide today to live your life the way that feels true to you. Yes it is scary and loved ones will try their hardest to stop you, but you must not let them pull on your heart strings or make you feel guilty. There is no guilt in you being you – this is what you came here to be – why would you feel guilty about that?

Looking at your life today, is this how you want to continue to live – scared and frightened that someone somewhere is going to judge you for your actions because you do not fit in with everyone else? You have a choice to make - you can either continue to live through someone else's idea of what life is supposed to be like or you can choose to create your own idea of what life looks like that fills you with purpose, joy and happiness.

Within you right now this guiding light exists, but do you hear it? Is the negative self-talk ever present with thoughts of, "Why me?" or "I don't deserve it," or "No one will like my ideas"? Do you know how to dial back the noise of the ever present need to make yourself feel small?

I once had a job I hated and chose to remain there for 12 soul-sapping years. My inner light was trying hard to get me to understand that it was time to move on, but I chose to ignore it. Its message made me uncomfortable so I sucked it up and stayed. What kept me stuck? The message of fear - to be careful what you wish for because the grass is not always greener on the other side. In other words, don't wish for something better because it doesn't exist so you should just settle. At this soul sapping job, I was just a number needed to get a job done – no name and no face. As a number, you are not unique. Instead, you are just like everyone else. Even though this tore me up, I decided to stay. I look back now and can see I was stuck in the fear factor – too afraid to move. I would hear about the offshore jobs, the layoffs or how bad the economy was which fed the fear inside, so I stayed put, which robbed me of my identity as a deserving unique being.

Within myself there was a battle raging. Should I stay or should I go? Put up with it and be happy I have a job, or set out to find something that soothed my soul? My heart was telling me to move on, but my brain was saying to stay. For a long time my brain won, but in time two gifts arrived. One, I was introduced to a life changing energy healing modality called ThetaHealing® and two, I was laid off.

Upon being laid off, I found a new job – where the grass was greener and they valued my uniqueness. This change allowed me to find my path again. I worked through the subconscious beliefs that were preventing me from seeing my true divinity as a shining light with a soul purpose. It was a grueling task but so worth it. I look back at who I was and what I have become and think, "Who on earth is that?" I don't even recognize the old me anymore.

Underneath all the beliefs that I had acquired from the moment I was conceived, inherited from my parents, carried with me from past lives, and what society had taught me was true; I had acquired a giant forest of trees (beliefs) – some of them good and some of them not so good. Using ThetaHealing,® I have been able to recognize and uproot the bad trees (beliefs) and plant new empowering seeds and love and attend to the good trees that were already there. I then water the empowered trees with loving energy of what it is like to have that belief manifest in my life with ease. Once the clutter and deadwood was removed, my forest and my inner light began to bring my heart's desires to light.

Now it's time for you to release the thoughts that keep you stuck in old patterns and harness your birthright to not only find and live your soul's purpose but to create that life you dream about – a life full of abundance, health, love and joy. Everything and all things are possible. Maybe you dream of being a speaker or a writer or an inventor, these are all possible if you are willing to find your inner light or what I like to call your inner roar in your own forest of beliefs.

What would your life look like if you could let go of the past regrets, hurts and mistakes and the emotions that go with them like anger, jealousy, fear and sadness? Can you even imagine what your world would look like without those?

These wounds that you carry can be forgiven, released and transformed into pure source energy so you can finally start to breathe and see through the veil of fear to see the truth of the world that surrounds you. Once you take off the dark colored glasses, you will see that the world is full of love, abundance and peace. It's all there already – but society does its best to keep us stuck by tapping into the fear of making a mistake or being seen as different. Part of your journey to realizing your true purpose in this life is to disconnect from the fear factor. This will be hard at first but soon you will see how much better you feel without all that negative energy being thrown at you all the time.

Once you have unplugged from the fear factor, start tapping into your intuition. Follow its guidance. Yes, sometimes it will push you to do things out of your comfort zone and no it is not trying to torture you. These are growth points – you need to do this step in order to grow into who you really are. Here the fear must be released so you can embrace the lesson. Acknowledge it, sit with it and push through it. Once your inner light knows you are listening it will give you guidance more often. Follow it – do not question where it might be leading you – just know that in time it will all make sense.

Keep following the path to your soul's purpose and know as you get closer your inner light gets brighter. Your confidence will soar and your inner tiger will be ready to ROAR from the rooftops! Here I AM and this is who I AM!

Tami Reagor is a Holistic Health & Soul Coach, Advanced ThetaHealing® practitioner and instructor, Certified Holistic Health Coach, author, speaker and teacher. Based in Walllingford, Connecticut, she is committed to spreading the word about how a change in your thoughts and perspective can change your world from blah to awesome! Tami has written and published her 1st book: Unleash Your Inner Tiger: Strength, Beauty & Power. Tami privately coaches her clients and conducts workshops and seminars to teach and help people integrate this new way of looking at the world into their lives. Contact Tami at tami@wellbeingis. com or visit www.wellbeingis.com.

Chapter 10

Life is a Journey to Knowing

MaryAnn Brouillard, RN

"You're never going to stop being at the beginning of your journey."
~ Ester Hicks Channeling Abraham

Life is a journey of self-discovery; a journey we have all come here to do. We are all faced with innumerous life events. Some cause trauma: mental, physical, emotional or spiritual scars that can cause blockages and prevent us from moving forward in our lives. It's the blockages that need to be removed, transformed or repaired for growth and change to happen so we can move forward in this Now. Life can be a collage of painful scars or one of boundless love and abundance with ease and grace. It's our interpretation that creates our life. We can release those scars at any stage of our lives so that we may become whole again.

When one starts their life's journey, one forgets where their soul was before this journey. Young children see the light of souls, but cannot express themselves by virtue of their development. As we age, most lose our ability to see the soul's beauty, or are trained out of this "knowing." My journey has had many steps of growth and many teachers, and my "knowing" stayed with me at an age when most children become "unknowing." At age 7, a very traumatic time in my life, I saw four souls at the bottom of my bed. They were dark and shadowy. It scared me, and I threw the covers over my head and said, NO! and asked them to go away; they did. I discovered if you don't want to experience souls, tell them to leave. It was a knowing.

I always knew I was going to be a nurse. I first trained as a nurse's aide and worked in the ICU right out of high school. While working as an aide I found that I could feel the energy of the patients. I could read their bodies, I could feel their emotions, and their pain. I could tell when something was wrong, and would help when I could. I felt energy leave people when they left physical life; I thought everyone could.

Right before nursing school, I was crossing the street, when a stranger came up to me and asked to see the palm of my hand. I thought, "What an odd thing to ask." Reluctantly, I stretched out my hand, he looked, pointed and said, "You have the healing cross." Studying the cross in the palm of my hand I asked, "What does that mean?" When I looked back up, he was gone. I took that as a sign that I was on the right path.

One of my first experiences with healing was with a woman in the hospital with a massive open abdominal wound. We talked as I re-dressed it and she shared that she was afraid she would never be able to walk again or heal right. I suddenly felt compelled to put my hands on her. With permission, I lay my hands on her abdomen. Two weeks later I saw her walking in the halls, she smiled big and said, "I don't know what you did, but LOOK I'm up walking." I was so happy to see her up! I knew I was channeling energy, but was unsure of how it happened.

I became an ICU nurse; I studied and practiced energy and the life not seen, using "Healing Hands" techniques by Barbara Brennan. I found my patients were energetically tuned and seemed to heal better as I used my nursing skills, modern medicine and energy healing. I loved the difference I could make in the lives of my patients using the wisdom of these three healing modalities.

As I thirsted to learn more I began to work with my mentor and friend, Dr. Fred Bader Ph.D. (www.TheLoveMovement.org) We explored near death experiences, communication with spirit in many forms, meditation, automatic writing, past life regression, clairvoyance and clairaudience. We read and discussed numerous and wondrous books. I kept seeking answers to explain the knowing.

My communication with spirit started to expand. I focused my work on automatic writing while in meditation. I was getting profound messages that definitely were not coming from me and not something I could make up. I experienced several past life regressions, and began my work with soul retrievals and soul repairs. Through my growing abilities to 'channel,' I helped bring peace to a family seeking answers to a friend's death, retrieved a soul trapped in the shadowlands following suicide, as well as helped a friend find a missing will.

The most profound soul healing occurred one month after 9/11 when I went to 'Ground Zero.' Grand Central Station's walls were covered with pictures of those missing in the attacks. It was so poignant and profound. The devastation was beyond belief; pieces of lives interrupted everywhere. There was a layer of ash on everything. There were huge memorials for the missing and for the fallen police and firefighters. As I watched, a large group of people were being escorted to 'Ground Zero.' These were family members of the lost souls paying their last respects to the place where their loved ones died. One cannot know how surreal, sad and unbearably heartbreaking this was to witness.

That night, I stayed at a friends' home two blocks away. It had been a long and heart wrenching day. I went to sleep, so I thought, when suddenly there were 100's of faces talking at me, all at once. These frightened and some angry souls were all wondering what happened to them. Each wanted to go home, but were unable to do so. One man was so aggressive that he said he wanted to come into my body and have me take him home. I told him that was not possible. I said, "You cannot go into anyone's body!" I then left my body and went with them and explained what had happened to them, the airplanes, the fires, the collapsing towers. They died never knowing what hit them and were now all lost souls. I shared that their families loved and missed them very much, and knew that they had died. I told them I could not go with them but they needed to move on. I guided them to a beautiful place that only they could see. It was an incredibly peaceful experience in the face of the tragedy.

I felt blessed. My experience at 'Ground Zero' was an affirmation that I was an open channel. The Divine chose me to be the channel, to spend the night helping those lost, frightened souls remember that they are soul energy, and they needed to move on as the Divine Beings they were. Their grief and loss was just as real to them as it was to us.

After this astral projection and soul retrieval experience, I did not do any energy or healing work for several years. This had been one of my struggles with the knowing, so I kept on seeking.

I was introduced to my next teacher Grand Master Min Pai. I studied Tai Chi and Zazen meditation at the Wellspring Zen Monastery for three years under his guidance, three days a week. He was a man of few words. He communicated energetically and physically and promoted internal power and spiritual growth. Since his transition Master Pai has become one of my spirit guides.

As I continued to search for answers I found 'Transformational Energy Healing' (www.Transformationalenergyhealing.org) through Kathy Raymond, a very powerful energy worker. I finally found a name for the energy work I was doing. It really was a journey of self-discovery, self-love and self-healing and understanding the "knowing." I attended classes one weekend a month for three years, with new healing techniques to practice every month and met my Earth Angels Maureen Goodhouse and Eileen Estra guides and teachers, and very wise women.

My energy healing gift was becoming stronger. I found that I could feel someone's pain or the energetic message from their body. I learned about fascinating and powerful energy therapies including and not limited to chakra healing, balancing, cleansing and opening, always creating a space for love, light and healing intent. I also learned to not take on their pain and discern if a discomfort or energetic message was mine or theirs. I learned how to tap into universal energy and receive Divine energy to channel my gifts of healing to help those in dis-ease, and accept receiving and giving abundance and Love with ease and grace.

Years later I became instant friends with Lorraine Warren. Lorraine Warren and her husband Ed were prominent paranormal investigators and authors. When attending events given with her son-in-law, Tony Spera, she always had me tell my 9/11 story.

Lorraine knew I was a nurse and that I could channel energy for healing. She asked if I could help her with her husband Ed, now very ill. I loved her so and helped whenever I could. On one occasion when alone with Ed, I decided I would do a whole energy healing chelation. It became a happening that not only let me know there was energy being channeled, but also stirred other energies I did not know about. It was as if a crowd of energy beings were gathering outside the house. I became frightened, and looked to all the religious artifacts in the room praying for protection for both of us, and to send those energies away.

Due to the strong and deep energetic connection I had made with Ed in those last days, I started to channel him. The following is a synopsis of some of the dialog from a recent channeling.

Ed is easy for me to channel, and he assured me it would get easier with practice. He stated, "I want to protect you. You are a pure channel." "I AM your channel, your guide and protector," I wrote, "This is so exciting for me!" He said, "You are deserving."

The next thing he said was so profound, "Soul Repair that's what you do, you repair souls fragmented by trauma. Ghosts are fragmented souls that need to take care of business and are caught in the shadowlands without knowing where the fragmented pieces go. The pieces need to be rejoined with the soul's whole counterpart...The Soul. (Our inner being)"

Ed asked, "Do you remember the healing you did with me? You stirred up a lot of noise from the spirit world. You were protected by the Saints, Prophets, Blessed Mother, Padre Pia and The Power."

This recent encounter has been my turning point. Now I have the understanding of what 'Soul Repair' means. I know that I am the vehicle for Divine Healing, a channel for which the Universal and Earth energies can do their work. I feel the Divine in my healings. I feel their energy course through me from above and below, the energy to my hands, to restore ones' life force for optimal wellbeing of the mind, body and soul repair. I know 'I' did not solve the murder, or relieve their pain, or heal that wound or release those souls after 9/11. I was the open channel for the truth to come through, for the healing to manifest. I am the one interpreting the physical body, mind and soul's needs to help heal our humanness.

As a nurse, energy healer, a seeker and limb hanger, "knowing" this work is way out there on a limb from the norm, I have faced my fears and doubts. I have worked through many struggles and vulnerabilities as well to find answers not only to help myself but to help those in dis-ease. I have healed old scars and have found unconditional love and am ready to move forward into my next phase of Now.

Life is a journey to "knowing." This has been my journey and now as it continues, I am ready to share my "knowing." Let me guide your footsteps along your journey. An exciting adventure still lies ahead and together we can "know" and 'Feel the Heal.'

"This is where your book begins; the rest is still unwritten."

~ Natasha Bettington

MaryAnn Brouillard developed 'SoulRepair' Energy Healing, a symphony of hands on healing techniques which supports the body's natural state of energetic balance. Working with the energy centers (Chakras), channeling Divine, Universal and Earth Energy, to restore one's life force to optimal well-being of the Mind, Body and SoulRepair. She is a Registered Nurse with a diverse career in adult medicine and alternative healing modalities and is pursuing a Master of Arts Degree in Integrative Health and Healing at The Graduate Institute, and has a BSN in Nursing at the University of Bridgeport. She attended three years of study at the Center for Healing and became certified in Transformational Energy Healing and its Teaching Program, a Reiki practitioner, Holistic Health Practitioner (CHHP) certified by the American Association of Drugless Practitioners (AADP), and member of American Holistic Nurses Association. Contact MaryAnn at Soulrepair11@gmail.com.

Chapter 11

Vibrational Essences:
Transformational Healing
through the Power of Nature

Susan Draffan, MA

L ife was magical when I was a small girl. Together with my three soul mates – my family's dachshund, my pet rabbit, and my invisible friend – I explored the numinous worlds of big trees and deep lake waters. Then the magic stopped, and I became lost. It was a long and arduous odyssey to find my way back to myself, but now it all makes sense, feels right, and brings me happiness.

This is my tale of healing, of coming home to myself and finding my place in the world. Though the details are personal, it is a quintessential human story – the quest for our personal truth and destiny, a soul's pilgrimage in the context of a lifetime on earth.

Childhood Magic

In many ways, my childhood was idyllic. We lived in the countryside and I was free to wander in the woods where the leprechauns lived and daffodils nodded with cosmic mysteries. Chestnuts dropped smooth buckeyes that I collected for the secrets they held within. Summers at a lake brought water spirits rising from unseen depths, stone spirits, birch and pine sentries, and a majestic golden deer figure high atop sandstone cliffs who imparted gentle blessings on us as we floated by.

Of course I wasn't always in a fanciful state, but the adult lives swirling around me were fraught with intense conflicts, and my trio of companions and otherworldly explorations insulated me. This coping strategy served me well, and left an indelible imprint on my psyche and my life.

Trauma & Separation

Life changed suddenly and irrevocably after a tragedy catapulted my parents through a divorce when I was ten. I was the eldest child, naturally inclined to assume responsibility, and had witnessed how crucial vigilance was to our safety. So, my subconscious decided to grow up and pay attention.

And with that, my inner and outer landscapes shifted dramatically and simultaneously. Family secrets that had long lurked in the shadows dissipated. One by one, my treasured companions left and with them, the ethereal magic that had sheltered and sustained me vanished too.

A predator killed my rabbit. My invisible friend disappeared abruptly and without warning. We moved to a suburban house in a distant town, leaving behind my gateways to the hidden ways. Shortly afterward, although she tried with all her might not to leave me, my infinitely devoted canine sister died. I didn't get the chance to say good-bye to any of them. My family tried to console me, but they did not understand or share the depth of my grief. I felt utterly bereft and unbearably alone.

Regardless, life carried on, and school became my escape. As I busied myself in the outer world, my shock and pain became submerged deep down, along with valued memories of hidden dimensions. I forgot all about life's magical possibilities, and I lost track of my essential self.

Decades passed before I heard the term "soul loss" or understood that was what had happened to me. My core identity had departed along with my companions and portals to the subtle spheres. My tender heart was shattered, and my spirit took flight for happier ground. Life proceeded to carry me further and further astray, and the journey home to myself would be a long and convoluted one.

Lost Years

Lacking an inner compass, I floundered into adulthood. I was restless and unfocused, frequently changing course and moving around in pursuit of something I couldn't define. Decades of academia and a career as a medical clinician and counselor in urban university and medical settings ensued. While I appreciated the rewards of helping patients and receiving promotions, my days felt increasingly dull and draining. In efforts to assuage my discontentment, I kept relocating, leaving jobs, relationships, and temporary homes in my wake.

The still, small voice inside of me wondered if there wasn't more to life as my misery mounted with the passing years. I was lost on the inside, even though I appeared to be perfectly normal and successful on the outside until a bottomless, unrelenting depression swallowed me up. I finally had to acknowledge that I didn't fit into the life I had so diligently constructed for myself. Worse, I had no idea where I belonged. I came to doubt that happiness was even possible for me. I wouldn't have called it "healing" at the time, but soul healing was what I sought.

My cherished cats were my only joys, and I worried about how they were being affected by my despair. In the end, I was determined to do for them what I might have given up on for my own sake. And, as it turned out, they had the answers I was seeking. Just as they had when I was a little girl, animals and nature would once again shine a light in the darkness and usher me back into the light of the living world.

Awakening & Healing

The key to unlocking my long buried self turned out to be a tiny bottle of Bach Flower Rescue Remedy (a combination flower essence formula for crises). I'd purchased it in hopes it would give my feral cat Charlie some relief from what was for him a terrifying medical procedure. But its astonishing benefits transformed both our lives. It taught Charlie that veterinary intervention isn't always abusive. And it introduced me to the miracle of flower essences, resolving my soul sickness and revealing my place and life purpose in the process.

My instant fascination with essences quickly buoyed me up out of my longstanding depression. For the first time I could recall, life was enchanting as I started researching the few essence resources available at that time. Fledgling successes with my own cats convinced acquaintances to accept my offers to help their animals too. The metropolis we lived in was huge and my time and energy limited, so meeting their animals in person wasn't feasible. Instead, I would sit quietly at home and reach out to them from my heart, wherever they lived across the city.

To my absolute surprise and delight, I began to hear them respond to my silent inquiries, telling me how they felt and what they needed. Equally wondrous, the flowers started speaking up too – practically jumping up and down in front of me in their little bottles, proclaiming how they could help this dog or that cat feel better. I didn't remember hearing my pets or nature spirits during childhood, but the messages flowing in now were clear as bells. My heart was singing, because at long last, I had discovered something I really wanted to do with my life. Glimpsing my soul blueprint changed everything.

And so began my personal healing journey. My subtle sensitivities were gently reawakened as essences lifted away the layers of shock, trauma, fear, confusion and distress embedded within me. As they repaired and stabilized my energy field, I started to feel safe in the world in ways I never had before. Slowly but surely, the pieces of my soul that had broken away so long ago began returning to me. I was on my way to wholeness and life was magical again.

Signs & Destiny

When we align our intention, will, and actions with our soul plan, all manner of synchronicities and miracles occur to help us reach our destiny. I yearned to focus solely on essences, but retained some clinical work due to financial insecurity and lack of confidence. Then one morning, I received an unmistakable wake up call in the form of a serious car accident on my way to work; it forced me to realize my soul would literally shrivel up and die if I didn't turn my life around in the direction my heart was facing. My only option was to forge a total commitment to my calling. Once I did, universal intelligence stepped in immediately to help me along.

A serious family situation resolved, freeing me to move away. I sold my residence quickly despite a weak real estate market, retired from my medical positions without further hesitation, and moved across the country to a light-filled valley surrounded by wilderness. Along with inspiration and growth, anguishing hardships and losses were to follow, and essences proved their merit as my cats and I navigated onward.

With hindsight, now I can spot the many signposts arranged to guide me through my years of struggle, though I didn't recognize them as such at the time. Unicorns nourished my innate sense of mysticism. Spirit guides held doorways to the subtle realms ajar for me. Lapidary and goldsmithing hobbies presaged my crystal and alchemy affinities. An electrifying encounter with an owl initiated my seership abilities. Reiki attunements introduced the dwarf guide who steadies my earthen connections. And, eventually, I realized that my invisible childhood friend had been an elf – a revelation that certainly explained our forays into the hidden realms!

Signs continue to affirm my direction and expand my awareness. Gnomes appear to encourage my work in the wild places, auspicious flowers spontaneously appear in my garden just when they can help me, allies appear in my dreams and meditations. The magic occurs in other places, too. One day, the spirit of Joan of Arc sent a sword of light into my essence bowl as I sat meditating in a garden where she was once imprisoned.

I am still healing and evolving as my path continues to unfold. I don't yet know all the places that the Great Mystery of life will take me. But my restlessness has transformed into contentment, and I trust my guides and essences to show me the way forward.

At the end of his life, my beloved cat Charlie demonstrated the soul healing power of essences when he courageously extended his leg through the bars of his crate in an animal hospital to receive a catheter. His veterinarian was stunned, and all the more so when I told him that Charlie was born feral, endured years caged in a dark basement, and carried past life memories of being tortured in research labs. His life story magnificently exemplifies the power and potential of essences for transmuting our past and actualizing our immanent grace and wisdom.

Essence Basics

Vibrational essences are nonaromatic waters imbued with the life force and consciousness of flowers, crystals, landscapes, stars, and other forms made manifest in Nature. Each living form has its own divinely appointed healing qualities and purpose, and each essence is a multidimensional hologram embodying that form's pattern of Light within the cosmic matrix.

Essences are traditionally made by floating blossoms in a bowl of water while the sun imprints their vibrational patterns into it. Modern variations include non-cutting, lunar and ceremonial methods. The physical actions of essence making are simple, but in reality it is a complex, collaborative process wherein Humans, Nature, and Source co-create living elixirs sanctified for purposes of healing or evolution.

How Essences Work

Every essence vibrates at a singular characteristic frequency. They restore disabled templates within us by introducing their signatures into our system through the principle of resonance. They amplify our inner gifts, dissolve energetic blocks, resolve unproductive thoughts, feelings, and behaviors, harmonize our spirit, and reveal our soul identity.

Essences support our expansion and evolution, as well as holistic healing through the mind-body-spirit connection. They do not change who we truly are; they empower our ability to be authentic and present, so we can more easily fulfill our highest potential.

How to Choose and Use Essences

Reading their descriptions and noticing our intuitive responses to them are good ways to select essences. Either attraction or aversion is a key to probable benefit. Practitioners can offer guidance and insight, especially when relevant imbalances are rooted in our subconscious.

Essences are very simple to use orally, topically, and as aura or room sprays. With no biochemical properties or contraindications, they are gentle enough for individuals of all ages and physical conditions.

Wholeness & Unity

Essences are microcosms of Nature, just as we are. They remind us that we are children of the universe and illuminate our own essential nature. Humanity evolves within the vibrational web of the natural world, and our inborn kinship with the waters, soil, minerals, plants, creatures, sun, moon, and stars inform our wholeness and unity with All of Life. Essences highlight our unique radiance within this unified cosmic field, helping us cultivate our inherent joy, purity, peace, divinity, and destiny.

Initiated into the unseen realms in childhood, Susan Draffan maintains relationships with her multidimensional plant, creature, faery and cosmic allies in service to unifying the living worlds. She is a nature and animal intuitive and vibrational essence specialist who helps clients of all species awaken to their magnificence, purpose and divinity. In her practice, Susan draws on skills from her advanced academic degrees, previous career as a diagnostic medical clinician and counselor, holistic healing arts training, and Celtic spirituality studies. She is currently developing a line of essences in the luminous Ojai Valley, where she resides with her human and feline family. Contact Susan at info@ShiningSpirits.net, or visit www.ShiningSpirits.net.

Chapter 12

Healing is Possible

Karen Lemieux, LCSW

I slept walked through the first 48 years of my life. I was born to a teenager during a time when pregnant girls were shunned, shamed and sent away. I was then adopted by a young middle class church going couple. I had no memory of my childhood before age 13. I thought that was normal. Adolescence was rough, I remember that. By age 13, rejected by both parents, I was on the street, drinking, smoking pot, and having sex with older boys. I left home at age 15, an (A) student, and I flunked out of high school. I moved out of my hometown at age 17 and it was decades before I could drive through town again, I'd just drive around it. The memories of adolescence were just too shaming and painful. By age 18, I was pregnant and married. At age 21, I had 2 toddlers, and my husband left us.

The Beginnings of Transformation

After my husband left, I started working on a psychiatric unit and on my bachelor's degree in social work. I met Wayne when I was working at the hospital. He moved in a short while after we started dating. He was in my life for a reason. There are no mistakes.

I began to experience flashbacks when Wayne and I were intimate. When his face was close to mine, I would see another mans' face obscuring his, but I couldn't make out who it was. It was frightening. I thought I might be hallucinating, but it wasn't anything like the hallucinations I had learned about. It soon became clear that these were flashbacks. They started to come more regularly and could happen at any time. It was getting harder and harder to function and perform routine daily tasks because I never knew when they were going to hit.

My forgotten childhood was suddenly coming back to me in horrifying fragments. Over time, it became clear that the repressed memories were of me as a small child being sexually abused by someone. Eventually the memories revealed that my adoptive father was the perpetrator. My adoptive mother was just as dangerous. He raped me repeatedly throughout my childhood; she was sexually abusive, physically violent, verbally assaultive and unpredictable. A pregnancy ended the sexual abuse.

During this time when flashbacks came as regularly as waves crashing to the shore, I became severely depressed and suicidal. The emotional pain took physical form in my body; it felt like there were tennis balls being forced up my esophagus. I was bedridden for seven months, getting up only long enough to pull on a pair of sweat pants to go to therapy once a week. Wayne took care of my kids and my house and the bills. I remember getting as far as the couch one day, and spending the entire day curled up in a ball. I knew that if I got up, I'd carry out the plan to kill myself. Wayne told me years later that he was terrified to come home, fearing that one day he'd find me dead. He didn't know what to do, so he left.

I had a home and children to care for. The memories were forced back underground and remained there another two decades. I pulled myself together, and went on to work for St. Mary Home, as their Volunteer Coordinator. I continued to drink, a habit formed at age 11 when mother started feeding me alcohol to, "help with menstrual cramps." I began, unknowingly, to experience symptoms of PTSD. I continued to sleepwalk through life, functioning on top of a simmering volcano.

I then went to work for the Hebrew Home as an outreach worker and returned to school to earn my Master's Degree in social work. Among my clients at the HHH were many holocaust survivors, Russian refugees and American military. It became very clear to me, that I wanted to work as a trauma therapist. After 10 years, and now a manager, I announced that I was leaving HHH with no clear idea of what would come next. Soon after an opportunity presented itself to work for Vicchyka Shelto, LCSW at Asian Family Services (AFS) in Hartford as a trauma therapist, providing outpatient mental health services for survivors of the Vietnam War and the Khmer Rouge. For the first time I felt there was a presence in the world that heard me and effortlessly delivered to me what I had ordered! I facilitated healing for survivors of war trauma and experienced deep healing myself. I discovered Buddhist philosophy and became ravenous for the teachings. It just made sense to me.

My life's work is about understanding what suffering is, how it's caused and what relieves suffering. Buddhism offered sensible, practical explanations that continue to inform my work and my life today. AFS had a grant to study the effects of meditation, massage and yoga on symptoms of PTSD. I began a Zen Buddhist meditation and yoga practice, and I learned Reiki. Energy medicine was profoundly healing for my clients in whom the war continued to rage in their bodies, minds and spirits. I learned that talk therapy was not the only way to heal trauma, and sometimes not the preferred way. I would learn later that Kundalini Yoga is a healing that does not require talking at all. In my late 40's, while I was at AFS, the flashbacks re-surfaced and were worse than any that had come before. And so began a decade of intensive healing.

I Didn't Know I Was Gone Until I Came Back

I began working on healing the trauma with Shankara Newton. What surfaced were physical sensations, overwhelming emotions, thoughts filled with self- hatred that had been isolated out and re-pressed in the original experience. A child cannot survive that intensity of experience. I came to realize that when my father entered me, I left. To survive overwhelming trauma we leave our bodies, and temporarily put away the associated thoughts and emotions. Dissociation and emotional numbing are built in survival mechanisms well understood in the psychology literature. Going through life, out of my body, physically and emotionally numb, is why looking back it felt like I was sleepwalking through my life. Major aspects of being human were outside of my experience.

What I came to believe about myself and the world surfaced along with the memories. I believed, as many child sexual abuse survivors do, as my clients did, that it was my fault. I was told that I had always been and always would be, unlovable, and I believed it. These were not conscious thoughts, they were stored in my unconscious mind along with the memories, yet they directed my life and steered the ship towards self-destructive behaviors. What I believed about the world, made it very difficult to navigate it, to trust, to have friendships or intimacy. Child sexual abuse victims often have multiple perpetrators, and are frequently re-victimized until they are healed.

I, like many survivors, was not safe in my own home, in my own bedroom, or in my own body. I was by social standards successful, but chronically under-employed, lost jobs because of PTSD long before I knew what PTSD was, or that I had it. I had difficulty with relationships and addictions. I had all the correlates. It's amazing to me that I've survived intact.

Shankara was exceptional at holding a safe space, being fully present to the grief, rage, tears, confusion, anguish and the many dissociative episodes that accompany this sacred work. He also facilitated an informal community of graduates from a Healthy Life Styles class he taught, who would spend time together, hike, cook and share meals together. This community was part of my treatment. These were men and women, all committed to personal and spiritual growth, devoted to help and support each other and to be of service in the world. I had been isolated my whole life, fearful of men and women, never made friends at work. Here, for the first time, I experienced through them, what a good, safe man is, what a trustworthy safe woman friend is. They were my first friends and in so many ways, my saviors. I never truly experienced aloneness or isolation again. During this time, my son, Jeremy died at age 29 in a motorcycle accident. They were there for me, stayed with me and circled the grave with me.

I learned in my work with Shankara, not to resist so much, to create space and allow what is present. So I let grief have its way with me. For the first 15 months after Jeremy's death, I burned in the fire of intense anguish and grief. I felt like a statue standing in an inferno of flames. When the flames burnt themselves out, all that was not me had been burnt away revealing the authentic me, the real me, like a sculptor chiseling a block of marble until the figure inside is revealed. I lost friends who could not be present to such intense suffering. Things became very clear. I had no tolerance for smallness or bullshit. I warned my friends, if you come close enough, I WILL hug you. I can't hug my son anymore, but I can and I will hug you. Nature took on magnificence like I'd never seen before. All things in temporal physical form became precious and sacred.

We only know what we know. Until I began to heal, I didn't know that my experience of life was one dimensional. Life felt to me like I had a wet finger in a live electrical outlet. It hurt, and that was all that I knew. I never wanted to be here. I had one foot in life, the other in death. As I began to heal, I had a glimpse of what life could be. It was as if I lived underground my whole life, and one day popped my head up through the grass, and there was this whole world going on above the ground that I didn't know about. I looked around in utter amazement, like an alien arriving on the planet for the first time.

I was in savasana during a sunrise yoga practice on a healing retreat with Shankara and my new community of friends and an angel lifted off of me. She lifted out of my body, and floated past my face. I can still see her thick black hair, and I heard her say to me, "It is safe for you to be in direct contact with the world now." I cried, because I realized that she had always been there, between my dad and I all those times when I felt completely abandoned by God and man. That healing began the reintegration of my body, mind, and spirit. Two days later I was in a yoga class with my friend and teacher Kate Callahan and I felt the room air as it moved across my forearm. I was enthralled. I remember leaving my arm hanging in the air, in awe, just staring at the place on my arm where I was experiencing sensation in my body for what seemed like the first time.

I decided to be here and my life completely transformed. I was beginning to wake up and heal from a lifetime of abuse, first by others, then myself. There were many times I might have died. I'm not dead, I'm the most alive I've ever been AND I have completely healed from several life threatening chronic illnesses. I no longer suffer from PTSD or major depression. I'm off all medications, with sincere gratitude to Dr. Michael Dworkin, a clinical nutritionist and PhD Pharmacist. I didn't go to him to get off medications; I didn't even know they were a problem. Trusting my intuitive guidance, I found him and followed his recommendations and healed my body and my brain. Coming off an anti-depressant took more than a year and it was brutal. I will be forever grateful.

Someone asked me recently, "What motivated you to do the work required to heal yourself?" I thought about it, it didn't feel like a decision. I felt compelled to seek wholeness. Something bigger than me kept inching me forward. There was an insistent flash of memory of how life is supposed to be; of freedom and possibility, of loving, nurturing, nourishing relationships, of health, joy and bliss, all of which I enjoy now. I got a glimpse of a better life that was possible and I followed it.

I came to understand how to overcome suffering from my own journey, and working with others to find healing and relief. My practice has evolved from traditional western talk therapy, to intuitive healing that incorporates tools and insights from my career as a therapist, eastern healing traditions, embodiment, spirituality, and energy medicine. I teach Reiki for self-healing as well as healing others and Kundalini Yoga which is a thousands-year old science and technology of health and healing. I don't do the healing, the healer is inside of you. I facilitate you within, to your own knowing, your own wisdom, to your own higher intelligence. Everything that I do, empowers you as your own healer.

Karen Lemieux is a Licensed Clinical Social Worker, Spiritual Practitioner, Intuitive Healer, Kundalini Yoga and Reiki Master Teacher. Her life's work has been to understand what causes and what relieves suffering on the individual and global level. As a trauma specialist with expertise in child sexual abuse and war trauma, Karen has helped thousands find their way back to optimal health and well- being restoring harmony and balance in the mental, physical, emotional, spiritual and soul body. Karen views all of life as sacred and empowers us to remember that we are our own healers. www.karenlemieux.net.

Chapter 13

Strive for Five:
The Path to Successful Self-Healing

Andrea Frasier, RMT

S trive for Five is a term I use to remind myself to practice the 5 daily principles for living a happy, healthy, peaceful life. It took me over a decade to discover and implement these into my daily life. If I had known these principles as a classroom teacher, I can only imagine that I might have been much more peaceful, healthy and less stressed out all the time.

There was a period in my life when I was not so happy, nor healthy. In 2003 I was diagnosed with fibromyalgia, a chronic musculoskeletal disorder that is characterized by widespread pain. I had very low energy, had difficulty sleeping, and I was getting colds and other persistent illnesses regularly. I found myself exhausted, in constant pain with little energy to spare for work or relationships. At the time I didn't realize, (or should I say- I refused to admit it) that I was actually really depressed. I felt hopeless and as a result I resorted to various over the counter and prescription drugs, as well as alcohol and recreational drugs. After several years of gripping side effects and little relief, I decided to take a more holistic approach to healing.

My Journey to Health

An illness can be a beautiful thing. It lets us know that we have physical or emotional needs that aren't being met. I started to learn everything I could about the human body and about holistic health practices. I've been on a journey, seeking a healthy, balanced life for

several years now. It's a continuous, ongoing process. On my quest
to find natural cures for fibromyalgia and chronic fatigue, I have read
and studied extensive research in the areas of healthy eating, natural
healing, and mind-body connection. I discovered that the body has
the natural ability to heal itself. Free from fibromyalgia, including all
prescription drugs, I now feel happier, healthier and more vibrant
than I did 12 years ago! Through a combination of healthy eating,
Reiki and a deeper connection to the Divine and angels, I feel like I
have found the path to successful self-healing. I am so grateful that I
learned these principles and uncovered the pathway to heal myself on
all levels. It has brought unimaginable growth, peace and expansion
to all areas of my life.

I noticed immediate improvements in my physical health, including reduced pain and fatigue, when I started eating mostly plant-
based, whole foods. However, my life was forever changed when I
started practicing Reiki. After my very first session, it was as if a light
"literally" went off inside of me triggering a response that I can only
describe as miraculous. I felt myself beginning to heal on all levels,
beyond the physical body to deeper levels of my mind, emotions
and spirit. This new light illuminated patterns, thoughts, feelings, and
memories that I was holding onto that no longer served me. I recognized them and became willing to let them go. I knew that Reiki
was a method that I needed to explore further. I have since become
a Reiki master teacher and a Lightarian Reiki master and received
Lightarian Angel links and rays.

The Power of Reiki

Reiki ("ray-key") is a Japanese technique for relaxation that also
promotes healing. Reiki was developed by Dr. Mikao Usui who lived
in Japan during the nineteenth century. Reiki is a warm and soothing
energy that flows from the palms of the hands to the client, promot-
ing relaxation and releasing tension. Reiki energy can also be sent
remotely using intention.

Reiki is a simple yet profound form of natural healing for the
body, mind, and spirit. Reiki treatments are uniquely personal and the
healing adapts to the needs of each recipient. Rei means "universal,"

and ki (or chi), in Chinese, means "Life Force Energy."

Although Reiki is often considered a form of complimentary medicine, all healing is a form of self-healing. We must take responsibility for our own healing and take an active part in it for real healing to occur. Complimentary therapies can help to restore the body's natural equilibrium and balance. When the body is relaxed and in a state of balance, it can cope with everyday stresses and strains of life much more effectively, opening us up to receive the joy and health that life is ready to reveal to us.

Along with physical healing, many people also find Reiki as a path to personal and spiritual growth. For me, it was a catalyst for inner transformation. The Usui based system of Reiki is based on Five Principles. They are the very core of Usui-sensei's system. Dr. Mikao Usui himself described the Precepts as being:

"The secret method of inviting blessings, the spiritual medicine of many illnesses."

The Precepts themselves are 'keys' or strategies that anyone can, and should, apply to their life if they are seeking a path to self-healing and longing for a more peaceful and happy way of living.

The Five Reiki Precepts are: Just for today...

- Let go of anger
- Let go of worry
- Be grateful
- Work diligently
- Be kind to others

Usui suggested that mornings and evenings one should sit in the gassho (prayer) position and repeat these words out loud and in your heart for the improvement of mind and body.

In a Reiki Level I class, we delve into the meaning of these principles by examining and contemplating each of them, focusing on practical ways to implement them into your daily life. However, one does not need to be a Reiki practitioner, or even believe in Reiki, in order to apply these principles to their life. Anyone and everyone, regardless of your religious or spiritual beliefs, can benefit from implementing these practices daily. Personally, I believe that these principles, when implemented, can significantly enhance the quality of one's life on all levels. By absorbing these principles into my daily life, my life has improved in countless ways.

Practicing the Five Principles

By practicing these five principles daily, you will be able to let go of what no longer serves you so that you can find peace and happiness in your life and improve your physical health, your thinking and how you feel. Reciting these five simple principles daily and absorbing them into your life can help you reduce stress, dissolve anger, lessen worry and negative thinking; enabling you to live a happier, healthier life. You will begin to feel more clear and connected on all levels. Place your hands in prayer position and recite these five principles morning and night. Integrate these principles into your everyday life and watch your life improve.

Just for today, I will let go of anger

Anger at others, at yourself or at the whole world, creates serious blockages in one's energy. It is the most intricate and destructive inner enemy. Letting go of anger brings Peace into the Mind.

Just for today, I will let go of worry

Worry is linked to fear of the future and the unknown. Although worry is not always a negative experience, endless worry fills one's head with toxic thoughts, lowering the vibration in your mind, body and soul. Letting go of worry, brings healing into the Body.

Just for today, I am grateful for my many blessings

Count your many blessings. Be grateful from your heart inward. Inner intention is the important part of this principle. Simple things as saying thank you, a smile, kind words, and gratitude can enrich your life and increase your happiness. Being thankful brings Joy into the Spirit.

Just for today, I will do my work honestly

Support yourself and your family respectably, without harming others. Work hard on your personal development and spiritual growth. Do all of your "work" willingly and with a good heart. Working Honestly brings Abundance into the Soul.

Just for today, I will be kind to every living thing

Honor your parents, honor your teachers, honor your elders, and honor all living beings, including animals. Practice kindness toward yourself and others as often as possible. You are part of every living thing, as you are kind towards others, it is reflected back to you. Being Kind brings Love into your being.

It is unrealistic to think that you will never get angry or that you will never worry about anything ever again. You are a human being and stressors of everyday life will evoke these emotions. But the key to each principle, is staying focused in the present moment by saying, "Just for today…". Each day, in each moment you make the choice for which emotions to feel. At any given time, you have the power to change your thoughts and change your feelings to those of a higher vibration.

I believe each and every person has the ability within them to overcome and heal any illness, ailment or disease, whether it is a physical, mental or emotional challenge such as stress and depression. Reiki provided a pathway that allowed my true spirit to shine through. I have come to believe that Reiki, the universal life force energy, is the life force energy of love. Self-love is the key to healing. By letting go and releasing all that no longer serves you, miracles can happen.

If you are struggling with a health issue, it's easy to let it consume you and all of your thoughts. This creates toxic thoughts and chronic worry, which makes your symptoms even worse. Whether you choose to experience a Reiki session, or become a practitioner or not is up to you. There are many pathways to healing. For me, this is the path that had the most profound impact on my overall health and wellbeing so I am passionate about sharing it with as many people as possible. You can begin today simply by citing these five principles and integrating them into your daily life. I promise if you do, you will see great improvements.

You can become an instrument of this powerful healing, loving energy by implementing these principles daily. You will not only begin healing yourself, but your presence will also positively impact everyone you come in contact with. So, each day, I hope you will Strive for Five. My wish is that everyone who is seeking a happier, healthier and more peaceful life will find the path that is just right for them. I wish you many blessings on your journey.

Andrea Frasier, RMT, is a down to Earth spiritual teacher and guide. She is a compassionate Reiki master teacher, transformational coach, author, and certified crystal healer. Her innate ability to connect with clients and help them find their inner-healer, sets her apart in the field of energy healing. Andrea believes that we all have a healer within us, and she is determined to help others find it! She holds a Master's degree in education, is a National Board certified teacher, Reiki master teacher, and angel card reader with life-long studies in energy healing, chakra balancing, crystal healing, connecting with angels, A Course in Miracles, and Ho'oponopono. Her healing methods include Reiki, including the higher, more ethereal vibration of Lightarian Reiki, crystals, and angel therapy. She provides useful insights and tips about all of these topics on her blog at www.AndreaFrasier.com.

Chapter 14

My Hands Led Me Here

Dan Lupacchino, LMT

S ome of us get the call to healing in our later years, and for some that call comes earlier in life. As a sickly kid with poor digestion and a variety of health issues, I was drawn to holistic medicine at age 16. "Healer" was the last thing on my mind when I sought out my first energy medicine session, but this initial experience left me feeling physically different. I knew immediately that this holistic avenue could help me, and I wanted to learn more. Unfortunately, everyone I asked said I was too young. It took me seven months of searching to find a Reiki master who would teach a sixteen-year-old student. Since that day I have been in an active process of working with myself to unravel the mysteries of what it means to be healthy and what it means to be in service of spirit.

Reiki is a wonderful gateway into the world of healing and energy medicine. It is my first love and will always have a special place in my healing tool kit. Reiki opened many doors for me and brought me to my work with the angels. A year and half into my Reiki trainings I came to a realization about emotions that many of us come to in striving to help ourselves heal. I realized that my digestion problems were caused by my inability to digest my own emotions. I was dealing with all of the normal growing pains, the stressors of peer competition, the navigation of friendships, the teenage mood-swings, the college hunting and the coming to terms with my own sexuality. All of the stress and unprocessed emotions acted like poison to my system, and I knew I needed to add something to my Reiki healings.

I contacted my Reiki teacher to ask for help. She suggested I come in for a session. I thought we would just be doing Reiki that day, but it turned into a moment that would change my life. We started talking, and I told her things that I had been neglecting to tell myself. I shared my deepest fears, worries and concerns and word "vomited" the pains of my life. With love and compassion, my teacher guided me to the treatment room and proceeded to tell me that she was going to do a mix of energy work. She would be doing Reiki and something called IET.® She explained that IET® works with angels and that it helps to balance emotions.

In its basic form, IET® is a system of healing that works with nine healing angels to help support us in the clearing of emotions that are stored within our body. These emotions create dis-ease and stagnation to our energy field. If we have deeply rooted emotions that are not processed efficiently enough, they become a program, a script, or a belief. That energy then keeps us from moving forward in our life. IET® helps to clear the energy of these emotions and empowers us with various angelic frequencies to heal.

An hour passed in this first healing session, and I was blown away by what I experienced. I felt like the session peeled away layers of junk that I had been carrying deep within me. I was calm and able to think and feel more clearly, and I was humbled by the many angels filling the room. I could actually feel their support. It was a profound experience to feel angels working so intensely to heal, and I wanted more of that kind of moment. I knew I needed to learn more about IET.®

My study helped deepen my connection to the angelic realm and other spirit energies. Using IET® on myself and others helps us to align with our soul's purpose. It moves us toward the job our soul is meant to do here in this lifetime and helps clear a path for us to achieve our mission. IET® does this by helping us heal those emotional imprints in our beings. With IET® we can clear our emotional program and write a new script. For me, the study and practice of IET® has helped to shift old habits and patterns and helped me begin my journey to free myself from emotional burdens. I have been able to live in a way that is in alignment with my true mission in life.

I spent the next couple of years, really honing my skills, practicing with other healers and learning as much as I could about the healing work. Just before the start of my junior year in college, my teacher offered to hold the Advanced Level Class of IET.® I was really excited to see what more there was to learn and to work deeper with the angels. I had no idea that my life was about to have a massive change. The advanced level of IET® course is really all about the individual. While you do learn advanced practitioner's techniques and energy theory, the level is all about the individual achieving dreams, reaching goals, and discovering and embodying the soul's purpose.

A few days after the class, I was scheduled to attend an IET/ Reiki share with my teacher and a classmate. When it was time for my session, it began normally. I felt the familiar sensation of the angels working with the practitioners around me. That changed in an instant when all of sudden I was floating out of my body and looking down at the room. Almost as soon as I felt that, the room shifted and I was surrounded by a blinding golden white light. I sensed hundreds of beings around me. I looked over to my right and I recognized a spirit guide of mine, White Feather. I turned to him and asked, "What's going on?"

He gently responded. "It's a window of opportunity. You have completed everything you have contracted to do so far in this lifetime."

I think some people would have to ponder this for a time. Being surrounded by all this energy and light beings would have been overwhelming enough. Yet, all I can remember thinking was, "I'm not ready to die, to leave. I haven't experienced enough."

White Feather chuckled. "You must know that if you decide to stay, you will have a lot more work to do."

The room couldn't have gotten any brighter, but somehow it did. I started seeing all the other spirit energies that were in the room. I knew I was some place different. I turned to White Feather. "I said no. I'm not leaving!"

He gently touched my head and told me not to worry, it was just a glimpse. You're being reborn. Then I was immediately back in my body. I jumped off the table, startling the practitioners, and all I could do was cry. I cried for at least 20 minutes. The practitioners later said they couldn't get near me. They told me that I was vibrating so strongly that they couldn't come any closer.

Eventually I realized that it felt like something inside me was no longer there, like it stayed with those beautiful energies. I was also dealing with the fact that I could have died just then, that something, some big heaviness did die, and that I was reborn. Later, when I was asked what it was like being where I was, I could only describe it as a mixture of emotions, somewhere between extreme bliss and extreme sorrow. Our language doesn't have words to describe the feelings. Something powerful happened to me that day, and at times I don't understand why or how. I just accept. It is my belief that my training and dedication to IET® practice helped shift and heal me to the point of being able to experience this spiritual awakening.

IET® has many similarities and differences from other healing modalities. It is an attunement based training, initiating people into working with these angelic frequencies. Although not the main focus of the work, IET® training and treatments help to connect us with a very tangible and intimate healing team of specific Angels. The system's training is also very thorough and provides great assessment tools to analyze energy blockages and help empower us and our clients to remove or shift stagnations. IET® works and blends well with other healing systems. Many of my massage clients benefit from using IET® to help release the energetic components to trigger points, holding patterns and areas of chronic pain. Although IET® works firstly and with the emotional layer of our being it is quite useful in helping the physical, mental and spiritual parts of ourselves as well.

I love teaching IET.® It has become a real joy and passion of mine to share this angelic system with others. As it was with my initial energy practice, I didn't enter into energy healing thinking I was going to become a practitioner, let alone a teacher. It took me seven years before I had the opportunity to take the teacher level training for IET.® It was worth the wait.

This journey hasn't been easy. It has required sacrifice and the willingness to stand bold and strong on the outside of what it meant to be a "normal" teenager. In the last eleven years, I've lost some friends and relationships, but through my explorations I have also gathered tremendous support, miraculous healings and deep wisdom. Much of this wisdom has come from my schooling in Integrated Energy Therapy® and working with the angelic realm. As an IET Master

Instructor, I continue to explore the mysteries of my own health and walk a path of service for others and myself.

Dan Lupacchino is a gifted healer, reader and teacher. Having started his holistic training at the age of 16, he has built his holistic practice over the last eleven years to include Massage Therapy, Energy Healing and Intuitive work. He is a Licensed Massage Therapist, Medical Intuitive, Spiritual Counselor, Master Healer and Integrated Energy Therapy (IET®) Master Instructor, recently being named a 2014 IET® Top Instructor. The scope of his class topics includes healing, meditation, metaphysical practices and spirituality. Dan practices and teaches at The Healing in Harmony Center in Glastonbury, CT and has published an article on Integrated Energy Therapy® in "The Door Opener Magazine." www. integrativemassageworks.com, dan@integrativemassageworks.com.

Chapter 15

Discovering Mana:
The 7 Essentials For Healing

Lauren Brandstadter, LMT

My great grandmother could read your fortune from the bottom of your demitasse cup. My grandfather said we were descended from queens and gypsies. Every cell in our body stores memory from this lifetime and of those lifetimes before us. Our bodies bring them right back as we become aware of our connection to the non-physical. I, too, have the gift of communicating with the unseen.

From the very beginning I knew I had to learn certain things. Memories of my father and I fishing, hiking, identifying plants to use for food and medicine and how to make a fire and shelter, all create a sense of calm in me. His soundless footsteps on the leaves in fall… wondering if I could walk silently in the woods like him. I learned things that are of almost no use living in suburbia. Dad had no idea how native his ways were.

I had always dreamed of taking a spiritual journey, and Easter Island, one of the most remote places on earth, was the spot! My mind was blown! I was eager to learn new healing modalities and soak in the culture. I was already schooled in Eastern, Western, and Medical massage techniques, and on deck were the Polynesian styles. The island also fed my unconscious desire to reconnect with my deepest self.

Rapa Nui's Polynesian culture and lifestyle supported my spirit like no other experience I had before. I discovered my ability to tap into "mother" and ground myself, as well as how to connect with

Source. Source is our divine inspiration. It is also our intuition. We are all intuitive. The whole concept of connecting to your higher self is ALL about listening to your intuition, raising your "antennae" and receiving! I tapped into my highest self before that trip to ensure I was going for the right reasons. I flew to the middle of nowhere to discover who I really was, what I needed to learn, and connect with the earth in a whole new way.

With nothing more than a backpack, a knife, and a few changes of underwear, I camped on the crater of the volcano, Rano Raraku on Easter Island. Unbeknownst to me, I was resting on a portal. The veil between worlds is thinnest at portals, and I quickly re-discovered my ability to communicate with non-physical energies. This was the second encounter since my father died that he appeared. He came to me three days after his passing. In shock, I soiled myself. Julio (my daughter's father, a Rapa Nui native) asked me if that was my dad, and I looked at him stunned. "You mean," I asked, "you saw him?" I struggled with remembering all my Spanish as he took my soiled pants and washed them in the crater of the volcano, all the while assuring me that all is well, and this sort of thing is perfectly normal.

I was living off the grid – no running water, no electricity, and no car. My transportation was a horse with a bad leg. I learned Rapa Nui from the cattle hands that came daily with the herd to have tea. They brought me tobacco, garlic and lemons from town. I was eating avocados, guava, bananas, papaya and lots of fish (Nanue). I did my spiritual work first thing in the morning. I climbed to La Silla, (a notch at the top of the crater of the volcano) at sunrise every morning, and chant Nam Myoho Renge Kyo, then recite Gongyo, which are the Nichirin Buddhist prayers. Chanting is a powerful engine for building a happy life. Evenings I left food on the fire, satisfying the ancestors while chanting evening Gongyo. I left behind all the trappings of modern life to reconnect with Source. I remember one of my teachers sharing with me that chanting is like polishing a mirror. The more you chant, the clearer we see ourselves. I did this every day.

Then I had the dream. The dream was after a big CONAF (National Forestry Service of Chile) employee party, where my husband worked. I walked down the maunga (a big hill created by underground lava) with chicken legs in my pockets for the cats that I had befriended. I had a few drinks at the party, and we decided to go home. I go inside the hare (house), lay down, and had a mild case of the spins. I decided to just be still and must have fallen asleep. The next thing I know, I'm standing on the bed screaming. The image was so real! It was a HUGE anaconda – cream colored with a muted orange pattern on its back. It was coiling around my legs, writhing up my body… I was scared shitless… weaving in and out of my legs… I jumped up on the bed screaming for my husband to find that snake!

The next morning I asked the old timers about the significance of the snake dream. All of them said the same thing… snake represents children, the unknown, mystery, wisdom, creativity, and transmutation. This snake dream was addressing a new perspective I would gain through the process of transforming and accepting the death of my old self. This process of transformation represented the process of entering other realms of consciousness. I discovered, and understood, that Snake would teach me to penetrate the veils of the Otherworlds. I was tapped into "Mother" energy and was receiving her guidance and protection. That dream snake showed me how to use my skills of sight and sensory perception by becoming mindful of my gut responses. Those gut messages teach us to listen to the higher wisdom that comes from being attuned, and balanced, on the mental, physical, and spiritual realms. Bringing everything into balance allows us the greatest advantage. Snake symbolically reflects the ability to absorb the vast wisdom of others and I was an empty vessel, waiting to be filled with all the wisdom of Source, of the Rapa Nui, and their healing arts.

I was changing. By giving up all the comforts of "civilized" culture, I gained a more acute perception of my environment and self. My intuition was sharper, my diet cleaner, my spiritual practice strong, and my body was full of energy. I was swimming, foraging for food, hiking every day. There were no outside distractions to deter my path. We all have a purpose that gives meaning to our lives. My purpose was to help others on their path to heal themselves. I found my mana in Easter Island, among the natives of Rapa Nui. Mana is the power that is uniquely yours – how you connect to Source and how you use that divine power. I learned a great many things over the course of my chosen career path in the healing arts. Massage was a vehicle to express my suppressed creativity. Spirit guided me to open my awareness. A Buddhist practice, natural foods, and simple spiritual "ways", strengthened every aspect of my life, allowing me to rise above the distractions of our over-stimulated culture to reconnect with my true self.

As my spiritual practice grew, so did the ability to intuit disharmony in others. Living off the grid amongst the Rapa Nui re-magnetized me. Giving up "civilization", and all things material, transformed me from Massage Therapist to Intuitive Healer. My work became heart centered. The teachers were not certified, or licensed, as the gift is in the passing down of the healing arts to the new generations. They did not need a piece of paper to do this healing work. They demonstrated their ability to tap into Source, taught me to connect with my mana, and how to use that power for good.

My aspiration was to be the best therapist, and healer I could be. I liked who I was becoming. I was gravitating towards other spiritual beings having human experiences. I continued my Buddhist practice, applying faith, study and all I had learned to my life. This practice supported the continual unfolding of my inherent potential for good, the ability to transform any negative circumstance into a source of growth and benefit, and a life dedicated toward helping others do the same.

After the birth of my daughter, we moved to Kauai, HI, which supported my husband's need for Polynesia, and our desire to be under the umbrella of the United States. I began my Lomi Lomi training (native Hawaiian style of massage). "Aunties" in the healing arts all shared the same advice: We are not in control, but we can vibrate at higher frequencies so that we don't suffer. With this knowledge, I realized that there is no healing of others if I was not healing myself. We are responsible for everything we think, do, and experience.

Seven essential things for your healing journey:

1. Have a dedicated spiritual practice. It doesn't matter what the practice is. Honor all that is greater than us, have faith, study, practice diligently, and with reverence. Be aware of your breath. Breathe deeply. Slowly. Take in the breath of life.

2. Ho'oponopono. Ho'oponopono has four fundamental parts. Step one is I'm sorry. We must hold ourselves accountable for our actions that have wronged or hurt another. Step two is forgiveness. Forgive ourselves and others. Step three is gratitude. We must thank everyone and everything that aids us in our journey. Step four is love. Tell the air and water that you love it. Tell your challenges you love them. Tell everyone you love them. Ho'oponopono is usually done silently. Sometimes, ho'oponopono is used as a spiritual clearing during difficult times for a clan or community. The power is in the feeling and in the willingness of the Universe to forgive and love.

3. Immerse yourself in nature. The best way to begin to heal, according to shamans of the Amazon, the Elders of Rapa Nui, and native Hawaiians, is to be fully immersed in nature. Shed everything you think you need, go into total isolation, ridding yourself of anything that takes away from yourself. Remove all the things that keep you from yourself and your goal of healing.

4. Eat well. Use food as medicine. Eat as close to Source as you can, nothing processed, boxed, or canned.

5. Detach from the emotion of an experience. Non-attachment simply implies not holding on. When we detach from the emotion of an experience, we are able to see the situation more clearly. Buddhists believe chanting daimoku and non-attachment supports the continual unfolding of one's inherent potential for good, the ability to transform any negative circumstance into a source of growth and benefit, and a life dedicated toward helping others do the same. Your heart will grow because you won't have the need to control. Watch the magic unfold!

6. Exercise. Engage in some form of physical activity everyday. Exercise boosts energy, reduces stress, supports cognitive function, improves your mood, controls your weight, and makes you feel great!

7. Love yourself. Create balance in your life. Take care of your body, finances, and home. Listen to, acknowledge, and have compassion for your feelings. Choose to be around loving people. Do work that you love and have a passion for. Give yourself love first, before giving it away.

I choose to dedicate my life to this style of healing because it recreates how I relate to the world around me. Helping others heal helps guide me in allowing or disallowing the energies that are coming in. How I raise my daughter, how I work, and the caliber of clients I draw to myself, have all been affected and influenced by my work. My spiritual connection, my desire to continue along the road of life's learning lessons, and the manner in which I present myself to the world are all outer manifestations of an inner journey, that from which my guidance and work are inter-related. Aloha.

Lauren Brandstadter received her Bachelors in Communications from Iona College in 1988, and Massage Therapy Certification from The Swedish Institute in 1992. Formerly a publicist for Psychology Today, Mother Earth News, and the Weider Publications (Shape, Men's Fitness, Muscle & Fitness and Flex), she has been a contributing writer for Holistic Primary Care, a newsletter for Alternative Medical Practitioners. Lauren is in private practice, licensed in New York and Hawaii. She has studied and practiced Medical, Western, Eastern, Polynesian, Energetic, Emotional and Spiritual techniques over the course of her 26-year career. As a Master, she combines these techniques for maximum healing results. Lauren lived off the grid in Easter Island, which transformed her as a healer, and human. She is an Aromatherapist, a Maker of Remedies, a Universal Life Church Reverend, and a medium. When Lauren is not in session, she enjoys live music, hiking, swimming, yoga, healthy cooking, and learning. Contact Lauren at lbrandstadter@gmail.com or www.PacificWindsWellness.com.

Chapter 16

Wellness From Within

Jill Myruski, LMT

As a child I was very connected to nature. I would go for long walks in the woods. I felt at home there. I loved the natural world. I found peace there when my home became an uncomfortable place to be with my parents fighting regularly. When I was in my mid-20's I had a profound experience that pretty much set the tone for my life. I went to a two weekend workshop designed to help attendees unload personal baggage so they could reach their full potential in life or just live a happier, more fulfilled life. It was structured in a way that would allow the participants an opportunity to become aware of self defeating thoughts and habit patterns and then release them. I had stuffed down years of pain from growing up in an alcoholic family. I had many traumatic experiences of things getting very out of control because my parents were unable to cope with their own lives. As a result, years of anger, fear and sadness was still trapped within the tissues of my body.

Throughout the two weekends we were guided to get in touch with our deepest feelings and let them come up and out in the normal ways that human beings are designed to do. Some of us cried, some screamed and some simply shook. Of course I thought this was really weird. But I knew that every day my back ached, my stomach was in knots, I had a tightness in my chest and I had a lot of inhibitions and fears holding me back from truly living my life. The process began by sharing. People stood up and shared their deepest pain. If you were too shy to share, you just listened. I was astonished by the realization that I was not the only one who suffered in silence. Listening to the stories of so many people of all ages and social status had a powerful effect on me, as I was one of the youngest in the workshop.

I realized that we all suffer and struggle. I began to feel compassion for the others and for myself. I was not previously aware of feeling this way toward myself. I had been waiting for someone else to save me from my pain. When I realized that no one else could do this for me, I decided to just let go and trust the process. It was grueling. We began at 9 am on Saturday and were not let go until 2 am on Sunday. Then we had to be back at 9 am Sunday to continue.

We spent the days doing guided meditations, breathing exercises, journaling and many different sharing processes. At the end of Sunday; in the wee hours; when the instructor deemed we were ready; we did a process to release fear. Everything we had done for two days and nights was to prepare us for this. We were in a large hotel banquet room and there were about 200 of us sitting in rows of chairs while the instructor lead from a low stage in front. For this process we spread out and staggered our chairs to have some room to move.

We had been focusing on fear all day so most everyone had these feelings out in their conscious awareness. We had to keep our eyes closed while the instructor led us to release a scream as powerfully as we possibly could! I hesitated at first but others did not. Many of the attendees were older then me and had lived through searing pain of losing loved ones to suicide, accidents and illness. When they let go, the ear deafening noise of that many people screaming was enough to set me off; I experienced my cathartic scream as well.

It was after 4 am on Monday when we staggered out to the parking garage. I got in my car and drove out. I was somewhere on the west side of the city, the streets were empty and the traffic lights were flashing. Newspaper vans were making drops. I headed toward the George Washington Bridge, homeward bound. As I crossed the bridge the sky began to lighten. It felt to me like the first day I had ever truly been alive. I drove up N.Y. State Thruway in total amazement at how alive everything looked. As the sun began to illuminate the landscape, the trees exuded a living presence I had never noticed before. When the sun popped up, I swore it said "hello" to me.

I felt completely connected to all of nature. I would like to emphasize that there were no drugs given at this event and I was not taking any either.

When I reached home my fiancé was in the kitchen of the house we were renting. He was packing a snack for some early morning fishing. I was glad to be home; it had been a long weekend! I put the dog out on the back porch and went upstairs to lie down. We lived in an old colonial house and our bedroom had a window overlooking the backyard to the south and a bow window on the west side. What happened next was beyond my normal reality.

I lay down on the bed and noticed there was an airplane coming from the south, then I closed my eyes to drift off to sleep, or so I thought. I immediately saw a layer of wood, then the attic storage cubby with a box of decorations in it, then another layer of wood, the next thing I saw was the blue sky and the airplane! I was getting close to the airplane when I realized where I was. The very next second I saw the rooftop and my dog laying on the back porch with a fly buzzing around her ear. The next thing I saw was the ceiling in the bedroom. I sat up startled, wondering if I had been dreaming.

Then I heard the airplane! I jumped off the bed and ran over to the west window where I saw it flying off in the distance. I realized that I had just been under it a moment ago and wondered how that was possible! I remembered seeing my dog so I walked over to the south window and pressed my face against the screen. There was no way I could have seen her from inside the bedroom so I lifted up the screen and stuck my head out. She looked up at me and snapped at that fly! I turned my head up to the sky and exclaimed, "I was up there!" Then I remembered the attic and ran up there to see where the box of decorations was. Sure enough, it was right above the bed. I didn't know what to make of all this. I decided not to try to figure it out and went for a walk in the woods with my dog.

As I strolled along a wooded path I became enveloped in the natural world. Trees seemed to speak to me as a light breeze rustled their leaves. I could see the energy streams flowing through the tree trunks and out the branches into the leaves! It was a florescent green. When a patch of sun shone on my head and shoulders, it felt like I was being caressed by the suns' protective spirit. I thought I heard the sun speak to me again! There was a consciousness I could sense coming from all living things! The messages were about love and acceptance. I felt like I had been transported to a completely different world! By this time, it was mid morning and I had not slept in over 24 hours. I went back into the house and lay down on the couch.

My mind kept drifting to people and situations that had upset me in the past. Every thought I had about being hurt or wronged became an absurd drama as I realized what was behind the other person's comments or actions. They were all acting out of fear! They were trying to defend themselves from being hurt again. If they had felt loved themselves, they would not have been defensive. Even though it was not my fault that other people had not felt loved enough in their life, I no longer had to hold onto any pain from not feeling loved by them either.

Since I had expressed such powerful emotions only a few hours before, all the energy in my body became unblocked. It was sufficient to allow me to become pure spirit, if only for a minute. When I lifted out of my body it was like hitting a reset button. All the programming and belief systems were erased. The only thing left in my body and mind at that moment was love! I continued to laugh a deep belly laugh with every situation I thought of. None of the old hurts mattered to me during this new awareness. I understood that we are all just disconnected from our true selves, which is pure love. This lasted for several hours before I finally fell asleep.

When I awoke my sides hurt from all the laughing. I thought, "this is it, I found enlightenment! I am only 25 years old, now what do I do?" I remained in that heightened state of awareness for a few days. I continued to see energy flowing through tree branches for a couple of weeks before everything went back to the way it had been before.

As they say, life goes on. I was finishing college and getting married, but I still did not know what I wanted to do with my life. Rather then have permanent enlightenment; I was left with a chronic rash on the palms of both my hands. The rash began the day after my out of body experience. My palms became red and itchy. When I scratched them they blistered and oozed then dried out and cracked. This kept happening until I finally saw a doctor who prescribed steroid cream for it. That kept it under control for 14 years until the rash and itching finally went away.

It went away when I began massage therapy school. We started performing massage on each other the first week. I washed my hands before and after each massage and I did not put the steroid cream on my hands. After a few weeks I noticed that the itching had gone away. The healing energy that wanted to come through my hands was now able to do so. I was able to express unconditional love through my hands. This is what my soul wanted to do! I had spent 14 years searching for my true calling and now I was finally happy. I could have begun healing others in this way when I was 25, but I did not know about hands on healing then.

After that early experience I always questioned the conventional wisdom in our health care system. I knew there was something missing. As a society we do not encourage people to go within to find answers. We run to medical professionals who merely do tests and prescribe medications. It is our immune system that keeps us healthy and free of disease. Our immune system is governed by our energy system and also by the way in which we nourish our bodies. When energy is not moving freely through our bodies we begin to develop imbalances and blockages in the energy system. This is when illness begins. Traditional medicine does not recognize this system even exists, however, there are some inroads being made now with acupuncture.

As human beings we are designed to express our emotions. Emotions are energy- in- motion, E-motion. When your energy is not moving freely, you are cut off from your spirit, your wiser self. Spirit exists in and of itself. The body is a vehicle for carrying our spirit so it can learn and grow. If we refuse to feel our feelings, we are not learning.

Jill Myruski earned a Bachelor's of Science in Business administration at SUNY New Paltz in 1982 and graduated from The Connecticut Center for Massage Therapy in 1996. She is licensed in Massage Therapy in Connecticut and New York and has been in private practice for more then 20 years as an intuitive Massage Therapist and Healer. While in massage school, Jill discovered she had a gift for feeling energy and a knack for applying holistic principals in her work with people. This resulted in many outcomes of solving painful issues her clients were having in their bodies by using hands on methods of massage, energy work and intuitive guidance. Jill discovered that she could feel a vibration whereever there is blocked energy in and around the body. She created a technique called Vibrational Release, that she uses to balance our human energy fields. Ever inspired by natural medicine and the necessity of it in our world, Jill has added Health Coaching, Holistic Skin Care and Aromatherapy to her practices, www.liveyourtransformation.com and www.bewellandbeautiful.net.

Chapter 17

Creating a Healthy Body

Cynthia Haas, LMT

Your Spirit chose to experience life here on Earth in a physical body. It is my intention to assist you to be the healthiest You. Our bodies are very intelligent. Think about all that your body does to keep you alive and functioning. I learned to appreciate this when I was not well. By learning, listening and practicing what I had learned, I began to feel better. How empowering to know that I could impact my health. It was not fast, but it was simple.

The body is designed to heal itself. It needs food, water, exercise, sleep, sun, and self-love to be healthy. Our bodies need a wholesome, nutritious and balanced diet. The best way to stay healthy is to not buy unhealthy food. It is easier to resist buying it than to resist eating it. So many of us learned to focus on perceived flaws of our body. Our ideals of beauty are unrealistic and self-defeating. Your body hears this and takes it to heart. Imagine being a child and being told repeatedly that you are fat, not smart or beautiful. That negative self-talk is damaging to your immune system.

I read an article on trauma in Psychology Today in the early 1990's. This article stated that one should be careful when working with clients who had trauma, as the trauma itself could resurface, and the therapist could actually do more harm than good if they were not trained properly. It went on to say that a gentle way to treat trauma is to use essential oils. The sense of smell is the only sense that is not interpreted by the conscious brain. Smells go right to the olfactory system and into the amygdala where trauma and negative emotions are stored. The amygdala is located in the so called "primitive brain," or as part of the Limbic System. This part of the brain is for survival and triggers the fight or flight response.

When I went to massage school, we were taught a course on Essential Oils. I began studying essential oils and using oils on myself and clients. It was not until 3 years later that I learned about therapeutic grade essential oils and that I really felt a major effect in using essential oils. My massage clients went much deeper into relaxation and healing. I influenced the massage school to switch to these higher grade oils and I wrote a course for them on Therapeutic Grade Essential Oils. These oils changed my life. I was de-stressing and detoxing, physically and emotionally. The oils work on the physical, mental, emotional and spiritual level.

So much effort goes into making oils that are therapeutic grade. There are four grades of essential oils. Therapeutic grade is the highest. Only 1% of all essential oils sold are therapeutic grade. To be therapeutic grade, the plants need to be grown in virgin soil and no chemical pesticides or chemical fertilizers can be used. After distillation, the oil needs to be tested for therapeutic grade efficacy. Therapeutic grade oil has a living frequency. It has been distilled at a low temperature and low pressure to preserve the frequency of the oil. This is what makes therapeutic grade so powerful. They are very concentrated, so only one drop of oil can make a difference. It is a commitment and a labor of love to produce therapeutic grade oils.

Each oil has a specific frequency. For example, rose oil has a frequency of 320 Mhz, which is the highest frequency in the plant kingdom. Roses are equated with love, which is also the highest human emotional frequency. We can use oils to raise our frequency, to heal and to just feel better. Lavender is known to relax and soothe the nervous system and is gently detoxing. I used lavender oil to help detox my body and consequently got rid of persistent allergies that had plagued me for years. Allergies, I have learned, can be a result of a toxic condition in your body. I was told by my allergist at the time that my allergies were so bad they would lead to emphysema, and that I had better get allergy shots twice a week. I did not believe him. I later learned to detox using lavender by putting one drop on my chest 3 times a day, and diffused lavender at night while I slept. Cats were one of my biggest allergies and I have had 2 cats for 9 years now!

Essential Oils are nature's medicine. They are the life blood of plants. It is equated to what plasma is to blood. They are 80 times more powerful than herbs because they have never been dried out, their essence has been preserved by skillfully distilling them which concentrates them. The oil is extracted from the plant in the distilling process.

Chronic Stress has a devastating effect on our health. The CDC, Center for Disease Control, says stress is responsible for 85% of all disease. There are two parts to our autonomic nervous system, the sympathetic and the parasympathetic. When you are stressed out, you are in the sympathetic nervous system, the fight or flight mode. Essentially you are waiting for a bear to come out of the woods and take you out. Your body is in a state of hyper alertness; survival mode. In the sympathetic mode, one exhibits shallow breathing, digestion is compromised because you are concerned with surviving not digesting your meal to its fullest. Living in a chronic state of stress becomes a habit.

The other part of the nervous system is the parasympathetic. This is where the relaxation response is, where our bodies know how to heal and recover from daily stressors. Many people, myself included, live in the sympathetic nervous system, fight or flight, and rarely get to the relaxed, self healing, restorative state of the parasympathetic. You can live in a stressed out state for awhile, even years, but at some point your health begins to break down. I have noticed this chronic state of stress in some of my clients, where they often cannot sleep or even relax without the aid of some substance, prescription or otherwise.

For many reasons, people are in a chronic state of stress. Overwork, financial worries, a sick loved one, too much to do, too much electronic stimulation, stressful job, boss, marriage, kids, the list is extensive. The key here is to learn how to manage your stress and how to de-stress so that it does not become a chronic condition and affect your health.

Simple ways to alleviate stress: These are simple techniques that can help you get into the restorative parasympathetic nervous system. Do either of these if you are stressed out, before you meditate, or before going to sleep at night.

Alternate Nostril Breathing: Sit, close your eyes. Place your dominant hand in front of your face, palm towards you. Close off your right nostril with your thumb, (if right handed) and exhale out left nostril. Now inhale through left nostril. Now close off left nostril (with your ring finger) and exhale out your right nostril, and then inhale through right nostril. Switch and repeat. Do this for a minimum of 3 minutes, longer if you can. What this does is balance the two hemispheres of your brain. The stressful thoughts are coming from your left brain. Your right brain is where your creativity is and your relaxation response. Try doing this before you go to bed. It will help you to relax and stop thinking. To enhance this experience, apply a drop of therapeutic grade essential oil onto your palm at the juncture of palm and fingers. I use frankincense or lavender.

Sit Quietly for 5 Minutes, Listen to Yourself Deeply Breathe: Consciously breathe deeply and pay attention to the sound and feeling of your breathing. Notice how the air feels coming into your nostrils, how it is a little cool. Then notice how your breath feels as you exhale, the air a little warmer. Slow your breathing down by making it deeper. When you are anxious or stressed, you breathe in a shallow manner. In the upper lobes of your lungs are stress receptors. By shallow breathing, you are triggering these stress receptors, and now have entered yourself into a vicious cycle of stress and shallow breathing. Conversely there are relaxation receptors in the lower lobes of your lungs that get activated when you breathe deeply. You can consciously reduce your stress levels by doing this simple exercise. It is good to take a couple of minutes each hour to connect with your body by deep breathing, listening and relaxing.

Change your attitude, change your life: Decide to be happy. Sounds glib, doesn't it? I could not have understood this years ago. Now I wake up most mornings and say to myself, "Today I am happy and am grateful for how blessed I am. It is going to be a great day." Gratitude is a high frequency emotion. It does make a difference in life to be grateful.

I used to be a master at playing what's wrong with this picture. The healing game is finding what's right with this picture. This is a habit that leads to fulfillment and happiness. I realized that I was judgmental about almost everything. If you want to rob yourself of happiness, be judgmental. I learned that being judgmental is a defense mechanism which protects you from being vulnerable. It blocks you from joy. By being appreciative, you are living at a much higher frequency than being judgmental and can develop a loving heart. This makes life and forgiving others so much easier. Positive thoughts have a higher vibration than negative ones. Happy people are most often healthier.

Many of us do not realize that we can develop discipline over how we think for the most part. It is a focusing issue. We will always have negative thoughts. We can keep going with that stream of thinking, or choose a different direction. Focusing on what you like versus what you dislike raises your frequency. These higher frequencies or "states of being" reside in the present moment. Thoughts affect your feelings, which affect your frequency. This is the mind-body connection. Thoughts and feelings are causal in manifesting what we do or do not want. It is important to be aware of what you are thinking and realize its creative potential. So much has been written about "change your thinking, change your life." Positive, non-judgmental thinking is a habit that has far reaching health benefits, and people will like to be around you. You will like to be around you!

Keep food simple, delicious and healthy: It is recreation for me to cook healthful and delicious food without spending a lot of time. Wholesome food is the cornerstone to excellent health. Today we are super busy. So many Moms work, and the food we buy is often not healthy. We have to go out of our way and be knowledgeable to buy healthy food. Large chemical companies have altered our food by making it genetically modified. Time will be the judge on the threat to human health. Many people have fallen into what I call a food crisis, where their tastebuds have been hijacked and manipulated by the food chemistry industry. Food additives make food tastier, can be addictive AND make you fat as in the case of MSG, monosodium glutamate. These food additives and flavor enhancers can be detrimental to your health. If the ingredients in what you are eating reads like a chemistry set, it probably is. Much of the food we are eating I do not call healthy food. We are too often too busy, too stressed and addicted to convenience and it is taking a toll on our health. We need to realize the real importance of the food we eat, and (for the most part), eat what is nutritious. We want to live in a healthy, vivacious body. Eating healthfully is a must. The challenge then is to make healthy eating delicious, easy and not another stressor!

You need a food plan. Otherwise it is easy to eat out or to cook fast and impulsively. New habits around food need to be born. It takes a little time, especially if you need to get a husband or family on board. I encourage you to go to my website: SimplyHealingLife.com for recipes and articles about food and health.

In conclusion, learning to heal myself was a process and now a lifestyle. What I think is important is the belief that I could heal myself.

Cynthia Haas, LMT, is a Massage Therapist, Kundalini Yoga Teacher, and Aromatherapist and has always been interested in health and nutrition. She taught herself yoga from a book when she was 21 years old. She enrolled in massage school and graduated from the Ann Arbor Institute of Massage Therapy in 1996. While in school, she was introduced to essential oils and began experiencing a major difference in her massage practice and her life when using therapeutic grade oils. She wrote a course in Essential Oils for the massage school. She is a teacher and advocate for people taking responsibility for their own health, not being victims to disease. Cynthia loves to see people get healthy by teaching them about essential oils, how to make changes in their diet, teaching easy breathing techniques, ways to de-stress and more...simple things that make grand changes in one's health if utilized over time. Contact Cynthia at cjhaas9@comcast.net.

Chapter 18

Happy Feet, Happy Body

Diane April

I see myself as in a dream from behind walking down a long hallway... I have a feeling of excitement... almost giddy. I clutch three books tightly... they are old, worn, tattered reflexology books. My massage therapist pressed them into my arms as I left her office. "Look at these," she said. "Find a class; this may be what you're looking for."

The following weekend I was in a small introductory reflexology class made up of what I thought was an odd cross-section of people... a musician, a public relations specialist, an aid from a nursing home, and me... trying to find my way after corporate downsizing. We touched on anatomy, history and discussion about technique. After lunch we were to put our hands on our class partner's feet. I found it magical... I felt a kind of connection I never had before. My hands were at home on a stranger's feet. How absolutely bizarre and right it felt. Before the end of the weekend I had signed up for the entire training course.

The closest I had come to thinking about feet before was my shoe size and where I could find a pair of red boots. Now I was immersed in physical body connections; the 26 bones, 33 joints, more than 100 muscles, tendons and ligaments, and thousands of nerves that make up the human foot. Connections here were previously made by our ancestors: meridians by the Chinese, marma points from Ayurveda, even theories developed in the time of the Pharaohs in Egypt. And there are the newest developments and theories from

111

the Danish, French, German and English teachers. The connections made between the feet and the organs and systems of the body.

The human foot is a masterpiece of engineering and a work of art.
~ Leonardo da Vinci

Connections were always of paramount importance in my life but were made up of friends strewn all over the country, family in New England, and nature. The nature of my childhood freely roaming fields and woodlands, my love affair with the ocean and its environs. It all wove together like mycelium…a living breathing loving network.

And now the magic that is our human form was beginning to weave itself into that network for me.

The Beginnings

Reflexology has its origins in China, Russia, India and Egypt. The modality as we know it today in the United States was developed by a woman from New York state, Eunice Ingham, who traveled to England to work with two American doctors who were working on zone therapy. This expanded her knowledge as a physical therapist and through trial and error created a map of the feet showing the reflex locations of all the organs in the body as well as the skeletal structure. Today there are many maps of the feet, every teacher tweaks their own map as their intuition guides them and each practitioner finds what is true for them as they work. Now there are practitioners on every continent with teachers who have created their own specialties: nerve reflexology based on the research on the pathophysiology of pain; facial reflexology combines ancient medical traditions with modern neuro-anatomy to help improve underlying imbalances; and cranio-sacral reflexology balances the energy between the feet and the head, interpreting the cranio-sacral fluid and rhythm. These are but a few of the specialties.

Reflexology is a method of waking up the healing powers of the body, stimulating the neural pathways through pressure on and manipulation of reflexes corresponding to the organs and systems of the body. Working on the feet or hands, this therapeutic touch can make someone not only feel better but also affect a healing response. Practitioners learn to perceive dysfunction when palpating specific reflex points, however, reflexologists do not diagnose.

The word healing had come into my vocabulary. I spent an overnight with a best friend from childhood; she shared that she had just taken a Reiki class and wanted to try it on me. Before she had finished the first few positions, I was amazed as I entered a place of peace and calm and wonder. It felt like the safe place of my child-hood…my woods, my fields, my earth and sky. Within a few short weeks I was signed up for my first Reiki class which I took with my friend and then we moved on to the next Reiki level, loving every minute of our new awakening. During the next few years my Reiki was just for me, my own spiritual healing practice and I was devoted to it. The door had been opened to energy and touch.

In the days of my corporate life I was getting a massage every couple of weeks; body and soul needed it with the stress as a Business Manager at Forbes Magazine combined with my husband's health issues. I had found the perfect therapist and we formed a bond over the years; we were separately navigating the deep waters of grief and loss. And she was the catalyst… pressing reflexology books into my hands and planting the seed to take a class.

An aspect of certification with the American Reflexology Certification Board is documentation with clients. This pool of people who kindly volunteered their feet became my first clients, and through word of mouth, my business grew. I took advantage of opportunities in the community as they came up and over the years they were wide ranging….the men and women of the FDNY after 9/11; the Initiatives for Women with Disabilities program at the Hospital for Joint Disease; the wild women of the Gotham Girls Roller Derby and currently the families at the Ronald McDonald House of the Hudson Valley.

And then another door opened…a local Hospice was looking for a reflexologist. Most of the clients were elderly; I had grown up with my grandmother and her friends and always had a special bond with the elderly. As in life, so too in death each client brought a new set of circumstances, a new set of physical and emotional challenges. Somehow I was emotionally equipped to be with these individuals

during their last journey. It opened my heart, and I began to understand the concept of holding space for another person, especially at
this life crossroad. It is still amazing to me what joy can be found in
this space.

Reflexology can relieve anxiety; this is a wonderful modality for
the hospice client since many suffer from fear, anxiety, and depression. As I worked with this population I became more interested in
how to assist as the actual time of transition drew close. Reaching
out to others in the community I discovered a technique called Clear
Light Meditation. It is a powerful method to quiet the mind for anyone, but it is extremely effective with those in transition…it combines a breathing technique with a chant designed to align with the
client's beliefs. As I have told families of my clients, I am not alone
when I come to see their beloveds. Spirit, Angels and Guides come to
assist too.

New Connections

My next connection, or I should say re-connection, would be
to Heaven and Earth. In September 2011, I joined 16 other seekers
on a trip to Sedona, Arizona with a spiritual guide. I was looking
and longing for a personal shift, something more in my life as well
as experience the joy of daily hikes in a spectacular setting. I had a
knowing that this trip would be extraordinary. The first sunrise hike
brought me back in time once again to my childhood ramblings. My
happy place with my feet firmly planted on the earth and the energy
of the Universe palpable. I was beginning to see the pattern; whenever I spent quality time in nature, all seemed right in my world. I'm
that sort that can watch an ant moving a leaf for an hour or listen
endlessly to surf hitting the beach…I'm a nature junky.

I had the opportunity to do reflexology on some of the attendees…their vibrations were heightened and their energies shifting…
and I found myself connecting to them in a new way…to ground
them and help them shift in the physical world…the magical connection I craved.

After this trip I was intrigued by what I was feeling in sessions
and the comments from my clients of the supreme nurturing they

were experiencing. The mind/body/spirit connection has long been talked about in the holistic community; research demonstrates that you cannot separate them in health and healing. A basic truth is that your body was designed to be healthy, meaning that you are healthy physically, emotionally, and spiritually. When all three parts are equal and balanced, you not only feel good but your life is happier and more complete. Asking my clients to take a look at their perceptions and beliefs, to find their connection to Heaven and Earth, to get outside and receive the gifts of Mother Nature, to eat good, clean food, to experience gratitude, and, of course, to get bodywork...this all supports their health and healing.

In addition to Reiki and reflexology, I studied herbs and nutrition for several years. This led to work in the natural foods industry where I had gained a reputation as a go-to person for information on what herbs or supplements to choose and what foods to use for medicine. My training at the Institute for Integrative Nutrition gave me solid grounding in nutrition. And still there was more. New doors of learning opened; energy medicine, intuitive healing, and polarity. In my quest for the new, better, best modalities to add to my toolkit, I realized that they are all connected. Those that came before have also taken bits and pieces from different modalities to incorporate into their "new" breakthrough treatments. So my heart is glad and I use what resonates with me and with my clients...the connection between reflexology, spirituality and nature.

At this point in my life it is interesting to look back and see where I came from and what brought me to this point even as I ponder what the next chapter holds. Finding spirit guides as a child in the woods, continuing unknowingly to seek my deep true connection to Mother Earth through landscape architecture and the world of herbs and horticultural therapy, finding personal spirituality through Reiki, opening my senses to the body through reflexology, and waking up to the larger realm of energetic healing, connecting Heaven and Earth.

Diane April is a nationally certified Reflexologist. Her holistic training began in 1999 when she took her first Reiki workshops. To maintain her passionate connection to the natural world, Diane studied Horticultural Therapy at the New York Botanical Garden. In 2003 she trained at the Laura Norman Reflexology

115

Center and then graduated from the Institute for Integrative Nutrition. Diane maintains a private practice in Westchester County, New York; she consults for Hospice and Palliative Care of Westchester, and volunteers at the local Ronald McDonald House. When she isn't working, Diane can be found playing in nature, experimenting in the kitchen, or hanging out at home with her beloved Buster the cat. dianeapril23@gmail.com.

Chapter 19

Putting Myself First

Jiayuh Chyan, MS

I was born and raised in Taiwan. As a young child I remember sitting behind the curtain of the sliding door wondering why I was in this house with these people and what I was here to do. Soon, school started and I learned that I was expected to study hard and get a good job so that I would earn money, status, and respect. I did fine with that. In 1988, I came to the U.S. to attend graduate school, and in 1990, I married my husband (now my ex-husband). He came to the U.S. from Taiwan as well and received his Electrical Engineer M.S. degree. My ex-husband landed a job that promised him a green card and earned only half of the market salary but at least that enabled us to stay in the country. We bought our first house in 1993 with my mother's help when I was 29 years old. I worked my way up on the corporate ladder as an actuary. Life went on pretty well.

During the initial 5 years of my first marriage, we fought a lot. After that, I remained silent so that we could have a peaceful life. I kept telling myself compromise is the key to make the marriage work. I drove mostly between home and work. I rarely stayed late at work because my ex-husband demanded I cook dinner daily and to be served on time. My only friends were my co-workers. I got out of the house once a year to go to my co-worker's, provided I told him 6 months in advance. It had to be during the day and I had to come home within 3 hours. If I bought things for me or my family that he did not think were necessary, he would demand that I return them.

It was not until 2001 that I felt compelled to voice my concerns when he quit his high paying job. For the next 5 years, time and time again I told him that his voluntary unemployment was not acceptable. Nothing changed. I continued to cook, clean, and work while he did day trading at home and kept losing money.

As time went by, I noticed that all I did was stare out the window when I wasn't doing chores. I felt so empty and that my life had no meaning at all. After more than 6 months of tracking my mood each day, the statistics confirmed my suspicion - my marriage was the cause of my sadness. Even then I refused to listen to Debbie, my co-worker and friend, when she kept telling me that I was not being treated right.

In early 2005 I visited my family in Taiwan. It had been more than 12 years since the last time I went back. During that visit, my family spoiled me. Then I remembered the feeling of being loved. That is the first time I realized I can no longer stay in my marriage.

Two weeks after I spoke with the lawyer and right before he was going to serve my ex-husband with the divorce papers, I found out that I was pregnant for the first time in 17 years. My lawyer recommended that we go through marriage counseling as part of the process, since a child might be involved down the road.

We found out about the miscarriage in the ultrasound lab. It felt like lightening had struck me when I looked at the still monitor with no heartbeat! I hoped for a miracle that the baby's heart would beat again. Everything my ex-husband said during the marriage counseling made me see clearly that to him I was merely a cleaning maid, a cook, a safe sex outlet, a money tree, and someone he can speak Chinese with. The divorce got very ugly when he contemplated suing me for alimony, claiming that he sacrificed his career and moved with me all over the country for my career growth. On December 22, 2005, I was finally divorced.

I went into survival mode which helped to keep my mind occupied after the divorce. I snow blowed for 3 hours and cleared 15 inches of snow from my 450 ft driveway in the first winter. With celebrating tears, I proved to myself that I shall survive on my own!

The experience of buying household necessities to my own liking brought me a new sense of freedom. I went anywhere, at any time without needing permission. I started inviting neighbors over and making friends in the town where I lived. It brought hope to my life. However, I was also horrified to comprehend the degree of emotional, mental, physical and financial abuse that I was in during the marriage.

When I was not busy with everyday tasks, my own thoughts tormented me. How could I have been so stupid, allowing myself to get into this abusive relationship? How could I have allowed it to happen when I thought I had a good head on my shoulders? What was so wrong with me that my marriage did not work? Maybe the baby would have lived if I did not proceed with the divorce? In the meantime I failed the actuarial exam I had taken during the divorce procedures. I concluded that, "I had failed everything in my life at the age of 41." While all these emotions swirling inside of me, I slipped into a deep depression.

I started seeing Sharon Diaz for psychotherapy and attended a women's workshop she organized called, "Putting Yourself First." One activity we did was a short session of Healing Touch, Reiki, or Shamanic Healing. There, I tried energy therapy for the first time on Sharon's table as she put hands on different places of my body. In one moment, she put a heart shaped shaker on my heart and shook it repeatedly. I started crying without knowing why. I just laid there and let tears drop silently. A little while later, she leaned over and said to me, "STOP, STOP, STOP!!!" I then broke down because in that exact moment I thought of my father and realized that I had been carrying the guilt of not being able to attend his funeral. Somehow, somebody was telling me through Sharon to stop carrying this shame. It was so deep inside of me that I had not known it was still there!

In those times of getting through day by day, what I missed the most was my father's wisdom and support. All the mixed emotions and regrets were so strong that my heart ached beyond what any words can describe. The energy therapy session with Sharon brought all this up to the surface that I had to face. Since then I began to talk to my father as if he were still alive. This brought me great comfort and helped me in so many ways.

Driven by both curiosity and skepticism, I took the first three levels of Healing Touch classes. Each time, my eyes and mind were opened wider and wider as Jeanne Zuzel, my Healing Touch Instructor and Mentor, explained how things worked. She patiently answered all of my questions coming from my number- crunching logical brain.

I practiced Healing Touch techniques on myself regularly and found that it helped tremendously with my emotional turmoil, stress, and depression. There was so much love and support coming from the universe! It softened my heart as I regained self-esteem little by little. The number of times that I curled into a ball at the corner of the room howling from the top of my lungs became less and less. With newly found enthusiasm, I practiced it on my friends and received positive feedback. I realized that energy therapy really works. It did not matter that I still was not sure exactly how it worked.

Meanwhile, dating was a challenge considering I never dated anybody else, especially in a culture that I did not grow up in. I had a few dates, but nothing worked out. Debbie, my friend who is like a sister to me now, told me that I can't run the first date like a job interview with a check- list. I discussed my list with my therapist Sharon and she shared with me from a woman's viewpoint that a partner in life is what makes the relationship work. That was a pretty wild idea to me at the time since credentials was how my world used to go by. I thought about it and changed my list of qualifications to focus on the personal aspects such as connection, support, and appreciation. I held off dating while trying to figure out what I wanted from a partner in life since I never had one before!

My sister and family visited me in December, 2007. Watching their whole family together made me feel lonely. One night after they all went to bed, I felt this urge to connect and signed up for online dating. Chet, who is now my fiancé, responded immediately. I had a tough time trusting anybody back then. It also took me awhile to look beyond his education, income, and job. He officially got my attention after he waited months for me to finish studying for my actuarial exam. He was still there waiting for me, as he said he would be!

What makes Chet so special is that I can be myself when I am with him. I can tell him anything without worrying that he would ever think less of me. He sees me and loves me for who I am. He is my best friend! I would not be able to get to where I am in my life had Chet not been 100% supportive.

Looking back, I now understand that without going through the hardship from my first marriage, I would not have appreciated Chet. In essence, my terrible first marriage helped me grow beyond material values and gain the wisdom to recognize my soulmate through the connection of our hearts.

In the spring of 2010, I was praying for a friend's recovery from illness. It was brought to my attention that visions I received during prayer all came true and she regained health! I have had visions since I worked with Healing Touch which included conversations with my father, but nothing was ever validated. The confirmation of my visions from somebody else for the first time freaked me out. I also started hearing a voice telling me that I needed to get certified for Healing Touch. I was very scared thinking I must be crazy and I did not know what to do! I was aware of people receiving spiritual gifts but it couldn't possibly be me!

In the fall that year, I had spinal degeneration which caused severe numbness and pain on my left arm. I reached out to Pat for Integrated Energy Therapy (I.E.T.). The visions I received were so vivid I described them to Pat while I was in the session. I secretly hoped that she would assure me that those were just from my imagination. To the contrary, Pat encouraged me to embrace my gifts as they came. This series of I.E.T. sessions with Pat helped me so much with releasing fears and letting go of baggage. They showed me that I, too, can help the human race. I began to put the visions I received in my journal with color drawings and words. I stopped worrying that I must be losing my marbles!

I completed the Healing Touch Level Four class in March 2011 after receiving the guidance that the certification is for the people that I am going to help. Prior to that point, I constantly argued with "the guidance" that being an actuary with a good pay check, I had absolutely no need of getting any other credentials. For the next 17 months I spent time fulfilling certification requirements that included doing 100 sessions, charting, book reports, and case studies, among others. While doing all that, I witnessed how people benefited from the sessions I provided, and my passion for helping people grew. And yes, that insisting voice that I had been hearing for a year was indeed divine guidance! In November 2012, I became a Certified Healing Touch Practitioner.

Continuously, I learn from different teachers with different modalities. I have found a consistent theme: The more I know the more I want to learn! My experience is that there is so much out there we just do not know yet! Learning the Arcturian Healing Method with Gene Ang has opened up my perspective of spirituality and the universe. Completion of the Akashic Records certified teacher training with Linda Howe has helped me harvest the potential that I did not know I had.

Everything I have learned and continue to learn is serving to help me get to know me, to believe in me, to trust the divine timing, and to allow things to unfold. All of this raises my awareness and solidifies my ability to follow my heart. I can feel what resonates with me, which enables me to stay in my truth and honor my spiritual authority. I am now assisting my colleagues in forming The Akashic Network - a new frontier!

In July 2015, I retired from the actuarial profession at the age of 51 to open up my own holistic practice. I love to share the tools that I have learned to help people move toward a peaceful, happy, and effective life. There was no panicking about my finances or not being able to make a living with my practice. I know that when I follow my heart and pursue my soul's purposes of making a difference in the world everything will fall into place like a divine orchestra.

I live my life everyday by listening to my heart and learning what truly brings me joy. As I interact with people I practice no judgement knowing that everyone is doing his/her best in every moment. Difficulties and challenges in life present opportunities for me to learn to accept and love myself for who I am. Our life on earth is a school for our human self to embrace and connect with our spiritual being. It was not easy to learn from my past but I am glad I did. The person who I was that valued everything based on the external society standards was fearful, judgmental, and lost. I am at peace today.

Jiayuh Chyan is a Council and Certified Teacher of The Akashic Network, a Certified Healing Touch Practitioner, and an Arcturian Healing Practitioner.

Jiayuh completed certified teacher training at the Center for Akashic Studies. She is also the New Haven Chapter president of the Holistic Chamber of Commerce and a retired actuary. Jiayuh holds a Master Degree in Applied Mathematics – Actuarial Science from The University of Illinois at Urbana-Champaign. Jiayuh is sincere, genuine and compassionate. Her strength is the ability to speak from her heart, connect with your heart, see the divine light in you, and help to guide you on your path. Jiayuh's services include Akashic Records Certification Classes, Akashic Records Consultation, Arcturian Healing, Sacred Geometry Healing, and Healing Touch. Contact Jiayuh Chyan at jiayuh@jiayuhchyan.com or www. jiayuhchyan.com.

Chapter 20

Coming Home with Yoga

Cara Sax, ERYT

My senior year in high school was an emotional one. Not because of the typical girl drama, but because my boyfriend, who also happened to be my best friend's brother, committed suicide. My friend discovered her dead brother when she got home from school. No one will ever know what was going on in George's mind, but it was bad enough for him to choose to end his life on October 30th, 1980 at sixteen years old. I was the first person that my friend called.

I can still hear her voice in my head. "George is dead." she said, flatly. "He shot himself in the head. His brains are on the wall." George had left a note to his family apologizing for what he was about to do, and telling them that he felt worthless, like he would never amount to anything. He asked his sister to tell me that I was the only person who made him feel like he was worth something, and to tell me that he loved me. I remember wondering what I had done to make him feel like he was worth something. I still have the note that my friend carefully copied from her brother's last heartfelt correspondence. That experience changed me forever. I will never forget the pain that I felt in the coming days, for myself, but more so for George's family who would feel the loss of their beautiful dark-eyed son for the rest of their lives.

As I approached the casket at the wake, George's mother looked into my eyes and said, in a barely audible voice, "Thank you, George loved you." As I looked back at her, I could physically feel the gut wrenching pain that she must have been experiencing as she clung to the handle on the casket that held her only son.

Soon after the tragic and life-changing experience of death, I was off to college. I almost feel as if I packaged up that experience and put it in a little box that I intended to keep tightly shut somewhere inside my heart for the rest of my life. My little box of pain was added to again in the spring of my freshman year. I was home for a few days on break. I arrived a day or two before my parents were to return from a short trip they had taken, so I was alone at the house.

The phone rang late in the evening. When I answered, I knew that something was terribly wrong. My Uncle Jim asked for my mom, but when I told him she wasn't home he said to me, "Your Aunt Suzie died." After a long pause he continued, "She died herself." It took me a few moments to interpret what he meant, but when I did, I realized that she, like George, had taken her own life. I did my best to comfort my Uncle as the pain in his voice came right through the phone and into my heart. I am certain he was still in shock from finding the mother of his two boys lying dead on the garage floor, her head on a pillow behind her car that had run itself out of gas.

When it came time to decide what to study in college, I knew that being in an office for eight hours a day would NOT be good for me. The thought of sitting behind a desk was so distasteful that I decided to go into Physical Education to avoid such a fate. I knew I didn't want to teach gym since my experiences in gym class in the 80s had been pretty awful. Having to change into an unflattering baby blue polyester "gymsuit" for class, and then take a shower in a big open "shower room" with no privacy and a teacher who would check to make sure that you got wet, was pretty traumatic. This prevented me from ever considering being involved in torturing kids the way that my middle school gym teacher had. In hindsight, recognizing my need to be active and express myself in a physical way, was my intuition propelling me in the right direction. I wasn't sure at the time what I would do with a Phys. Ed. degree from Penn State University, but I knew that somehow it was right for me.

My sophomore year, I saw an ad in the college paper. The local health club was looking for aerobic instructors. High impact aerobics was the latest craze and I wanted to be a part of it. I walked into

Lady Nautilus and asked to speak to the owner. Looking back, I am shocked at how courageous I was at nineteen. I had absolutely no experience teaching anything at all, let alone the latest fitness trend. The owner came to meet me and asked if I had taught before. I heard myself say, "Yes," and then quickly made up some white lie about teaching the past few summers at the health club in my hometown. Luckily she never asked me for references or proof of employment. When she said, "Okay, come back on Friday and give me a demo class," it took everything I had to not say, "Never mind, I was just kidding," and run out of there and never come back.

I had to think of something fast, Friday was two days away and I had no idea how I was going to pull this off. I went straight to the bookstore and I bought my first Jane Fonda VHS tape. I practiced until I felt a reasonable amount of confidence for someone who had lied their way into teaching an aerobic class. Somehow I managed to do well enough to get the job and my career as a fitness instructor began.

I finished college as an "Exercise Specialist," and moved to New York City to work as a personal trainer. Before long, I had become a personal trainer to the stars, working one-on-one with some of New York's most successful, famous, and wealthy people. Although I still worked forty hours a week at my day job, I managed to build a very large personal training business outside of work. I trained clients in their homes in New York City and also the Hamptons on the weekends. At twenty-two years old, I got to see how rich and famous people lived. It didn't take me long to realize that although they were wealthy and successful, at the end of the day, they were no different than I was. They had happy and sad times. They had successes and failures. They were sometimes courageous and other times fearful. Just like me, they had challenges and heartbreaks. And they too, sooner or later had to face loss and death.

For the next few years, I helped many people get stronger and more fit, and connect to their bodies and disconnect from their minds. I learned that many people had so much on their minds that they had a very hard time connecting to their bodies. When they spent an hour exercising their physical bodies, their busy minds got a rest. When my clients confided in me about their lives, their struggles, and their joys, I knew that I was on to something. I knew then that exercising the physical body offered more than just getting in shape and looking good. The results went deeper. I noticed that exercising the physical body provided such a release for people that they began to let go of mental and emotional baggage that they didn't need to carry around. At twenty-three, I became more than just a personal trainer who helped them get in shape, I was helping them to heal all parts of themselves. When I was working with a client, I didn't give advice and I didn't solve their problems. All I did was hold the space so that they could begin to heal themselves.

When I found yoga, I felt like I had come home. At the end of my first class, tears streamed down my cheeks. It felt like the lid on my little box of pain opened up and it was safe to let some of its contents spill out onto my mat. Over the next few years, I began the process of healing myself. The more I studied and practiced yoga, the more I realized that I wasn't really whole, and I wouldn't be until I dealt with my "little box of pain." I was very good at helping others to get healthy, but I had been stuffing my own pain and sadness down so much that my physical body began to be affected. I had also been taking on the pain and suffering of others in an unconscious attempt to help them heal. I had lower back pain and developed irritable bowel syndrome. Instead of looking for an emotional cause for my physical symptoms, I would chalk them up to weak abdominals, or not enough fiber in my diet.

When I was on my yoga mat, I began to explore all parts of myself, not just the physical. My greatest discovery was the realization that I was a highly compassionate and sensitive person, which made me like a beacon of light that drew to me those who were in pain. I often found that even strangers would unintentionally unload their painful experiences onto me. My "little box of pain" had been an unconscious attempt to deal with all the energy that bombarded me on a regular basis. Instead of actually feeling the intense and painful emotions, my own and others, I avoided them by stuffing them deep down. I put all of my heartbreaks and losses in there. The suicides of my boyfriend and my aunt went in the box. Two miscarriages, my sister in law's death from cancer, my mom's Alzheimer's disease went in there too. All of my pain and sadness went in that box so that I could continue with my life and support the others who needed me. If I just stuffed my pain in there and shut the lid, I didn't have to feel it. It never occurred to me that I was also closing off my ability to fully feel the love and joy required to connect with others. My husband used to call me the "ice princess." I didn't realize how closed off I actually was until I discovered yoga.

Once the lid on my little box of pain was open, there was no turning back. Every class for me ended in tears. I hated it, but the release that I felt afterwards is what kept me going back again and again. I knew it was something that I had to do. Yoga began a process of revealing and healing for me. In addition to yoga, I began working with a gifted healer. Through process work I was able to release the pain, anger, and guilt that I had stuffed down surrounding the suicide of my young boyfriend. I realized that my feelings needed to be felt, good and bad, in order to be fully alive. Over time, my physical symptoms went away and I learned how to hold space for people to feel their feelings without taking them on as my own. Letting myself feel my pain and sadness opened me up to feeling more joy and happiness as well.

My love for yoga and helping people to become healthy and whole led me to become a certified yoga teacher and a holistic health counselor. I have developed a strong intuition, which I use when I am teaching and counseling others. Over the years, my ability to help facilitate healing in others has gotten stronger, not from getting a degree or certification, but by listening, feeling, and practicing. The most powerful lessons in becoming a healer have come from the work that I have done to heal myself.

When I work with people, I encourage them to follow their intuition and let themselves feel their feelings. Before they can do so they have to get in touch with the sensations in their bodies. The better we know our bodies, the more able we will be to feel what is right and wrong for us. That is intuition. You get a feeling in your body of yes or no. Becoming healthy in the physical body can be a vehicle for getting healthy in the mental, emotional, and spiritual body as well.

To be healthy is to be whole...body, mind, and spirit.

It can be difficult and painful to live in this material world. It can also be amazing and pleasurable. By pushing down the difficult and painful emotions that we experience in life, we numb ourselves to feeling the amazing and pleasurable ones. Becoming whole is an ongoing process that requires the courage to be vulnerable enough to feel both. To be vulnerable doesn't mean we are weak. It actually means the opposite. It takes more courage to stay open to the uncertainty and imperfection of life than it does to close our hearts to it. In other words, it takes courage to feel.

We all have the ability to become whole. Getting in touch with the body is a great first step to getting there. Moving and stretching or better yet, practicing yoga every day will help you to discover where you are shut down physically. This connection to yourself on a physical level can reveal where you have shut down emotionally.

Don't be afraid to be vulnerable. Let your emotions flow. Be authentic. It takes courage to face the uncertainty of life with your heart open. But remember that keeping your heart open not only lets in the hard to face emotions like sadness, loss, and loneliness; it also lets in joy, belonging, and love.

Spend time every day in quiet reflection. Sit, breathe, or meditate to connect to yourself and let your trapped emotions surface. Work with a healer or a friend that can hold space for you and be a non-judgmental listener.

Finally, accept where you are now and be patient with yourself. With love, self-compassion, and most likely some tears, you can begin the process of becoming whole in your body, in your mind, and in your spirit.

Cara Sax is a certified yoga teacher, fitness trainer and holistic health counselor. She is the owner of Elevate Yoga Studio in Cortlandt Manor, New York. She has been in the field of health and healing for over thirty years. Her Bachelor's degree in Exercise Science gives her a strong foundation and excellent understanding of the physical body when she creates her vinyasa style flow yoga classes. Through her blog, www.perfectbalancewithcara.com, Cara shares her thoughts, ideas, and advice on how to use the tools passed down from the ancient philosophy of yoga to deal with present day challenges. She is certified in Yoga Trance

Dance and has developed her own style of YogaDance which she often teaches at her bi-annual yoga retreats in the Catskills. Other certifications include prenatal yoga and holistic health counseling.

Epilogue

Isn't it all about what we learn on the journey than what's at the end of the road? I think most of you would agree after reading this inspirational book. But many of us are so busy frantically trying to get to the end of the road or "there," that we totally miss the journey. Wherever "there" is for you could be related to your financial, emotional, spiritual or physical goals. I hear so many people say the following things about getting "there."

"When I'm making x dollars, then I'll be successful and happy."

"When I lose x pounds, then I'll be attractive and find someone to love me."

"When I find God (or whatever spiritual figure you believe in, if any), then I will have peace and comfort."

"When my career takes off and I get that position, then I'll have made it."

"When I find someone to share my life with, then I'll be content."

I am guilty as well of saying the same things to myself. We all do it. But what I've come to realize, and then sometimes forget, is that there is no "there." It doesn't exist. Because when you finally get "there" in one area of your life, you'll just create a new "there" that is farther out of reach than the original "there." It's what we do.

We all act as though there is this final destination at which we can arrive and have all of our dreams come true, have millions of dollars and live completely and utterly in bliss. A place we can reach, where we can be "done." But we're never done. Done is death! Retirement is a fantasy. Ask any business owner who became a millionaire and retired. It probably lasted about six months and then they started another business. The richest man in the world is still working. Why?

Because he loves what he does. So if you're still intending on getting "there," find something that you love to do that makes driving yourself crazy worthwhile!

Enjoying the journey is a hard thing to do for many people. We're so consumed with figuring out how we're going to get there, what it's going to take, how much it's going to cost, how much money we'll make, when is it going to happen. How can you possibly enjoy the process with all of these things to worry about? The key is to cultivate a spiritual practice to allow stillness, peace and meditation into your life. When you quiet the mind, you are able to see the beauty in the process of where you have been, where you are now and where you are going. You may even be able to see that you have made tremendous progress towards a goal or a dream that previously was hidden to you because you were so caught up in the day to day minutia of getting there. This is when it becomes critical for you to stop and smell the flowers, so to speak. If you are not able to see the progress, you will become frustrated and critical of yourself for not accomplishing your goal fast enough. Taking the time to meditate and be quiet will allow you to see the bigger picture and feel good about how far you have come.

There are so many amazing stories in this book about spiritual practices and how these rituals have enabled the writers to find purpose, balance and spirituality in their lives. For me, a great experience was taking a three-day silent retreat. Not only did it help to ground me and open me up to new possibilities and visions for my life, but it created the space for me to really examine how far I had come in the last few years. I was able to acknowledge my accomplishments and I felt really good about where I was on the journey. The clarity and insight that I received after all the distractions fell away was priceless. Don't wait until most of your life has passed by to start enjoying the journey. It's all part of the grand scheme of why we each are here in this lifetime.

Diane E. Hayden, PhD
December, 2016

Suggested Reading & Resources

A Mind of Your Own; The Truth about Depression and How Women Can Heal Their Bodies to Reclaim Their Lives by Kelly Brogan MD, (March 15, 2016), HarperCollins Publishers.

Anatomy of the Spirit: The Seven Stages of Power and Healing by Caroline Myss, (August 26, 1997), Harmony.

Animal Spirit Guides: An Easy-to-Use Handbook for Identifying and Understanding Your Power Animals and Animal Spirit Helpers by Stephen Farmer, (2006), Hay House, Inc.

A Return to Love by Marianne Williamson, (March 15, 1996), HarperOne.

Ask and It Is Given by Abraham Hicks, (December 2, 2003), Hay House.

Awake at the Bedside, Contemplative Teachings on Palliative and End-Of-Life Care, Edited by Koshin Paley Ellison and Matt Weingast, (2016), Wisdom Publications.

Being of Power: The 9 Practices to Ignite an Empowered Life by Baron Baptiste, (2013), Hay House Inc.

Broken Open: How Difficult Times Can Help Us Grow by Elizabeth Lessor, (June 14, 2005), Random House.

Childhood Disrupted: How Your Biography Becomes Your Biology, and How You Can Heal by Donna Jackson Nakazawa, (July 7, 2015), Atria Books an Imprint of Simon and Schuster, Inc.

Conversations with God: an uncommon dialogue by Neale Donald Walsh, (1998), Hampton Roads Publishing Company, Inc.

Energy Healing, A Pathway to Inner Growth, by Jim Gilkeson, (2000), Marlow & Company.

Energy Medicine, by Donna Eden with David Feinstein, (1998), Tarcher/Putnam Books.

Feet First: A Guide to Foot Reflexology by Laura Norman with Thomas Cowan, (1988), A Fireside Book Published by Simon & Schuster.

Feng Shui for the Soul by Denise Linn, (1999), Hay House, Inc.
Feng Shui: Harmony by Design by Nancy SantoPietro, (1996), Perigee Books.

Five Levels of Attachment: Toltec Wisdom for the Modern World by Don Miguel Ruiz and Don Miguel Ruiz, Jr., (June 1, 2015), Hierophant Publishing.

Flower Essence Repertory by Patricia Kaminski and Richard Katz, (2004), Flower Essence Society publication, available at fesflowers.com.

Grain Brain: The Surprising Truth about Wheat, Carbs and Sugar-Your Brain's Silent Killers by David Perlmutter, MD, (September, 2013), Little, Brown and Company.

Healing Animals Naturally with Flower Essences and Intuitive Listening by Sharon Callahan, (2001), Sacred Spirit Publishing, available at anaflora.com.

Interior Design with Feng Shui by Sarah Rossbach, (1987), Penguin Books.

Interview with an Angel: Our world, ourselves, our destiny by Steven J. Thayer & Linda Sue Nathanson, Ph.D, (1997), Edin Books, Inc.

It's not about the money: Unlock your Money Type to achieve spiritual and financial abundance by Brent Kessel, (2008), An Imprint of HarperCollinsPublishers.

Living Color by Sarah Rossbach and Lin Yun, (1994), Kodansha International.

Mind Over Medicine; Scientific Proof That You Can Heal Yourself by Lissa Rankin, MD, (December 1, 2014), Hay House, Inc.

Money and The Law of Attraction: learn to attract wealth, health and happiness, by Esther and Jerry Hicks, (2008), Hay House Inc.

Money Magic: Unleashing your true potential for prosperity and fulfillment, by Deborah L. Price, (2000), New World Library, Novato, CA.

Nurturing Healing Love; A Mother's Journey of Hope and Forgiveness by Scarlett Lewis, (October 27, 2014), Hay House, Inc.

Radical Remission; Surviving Cancer Against All Odds by Kelly A. Turner, PhD, (March 18, 2014), HarperCollins Publishers.

Reflexology by Bill Flocco, (2014), Penguin Group (USA) Inc.

Reiki, A Comprehensive Guide by Pamela Miles, (2006), Jeremy P. Tarcher/Penguin.

Riding Between the Worlds: Expanding Our Potential Through the Way of the Horse by Linda Kohanov, (August 2007), New World Library.

Sastun: My Apprenticeship with a Maya Healer by Rosita Arvigo, (1994), HarperCollins.

The Art of Extreme Self-Care: Transform Your Life One Month at a Time by Cheryl Richardson, (May 1, 2012), Hay House.

The Art of Spiritual Healing by Keith Sherwood, (2001), Llewellyn Publications.

The Art & Technique of Using Flower Essences by Cynthia Athina Kemp Scherer, (2002), Desert Alchemy Editions, available at desert-alchemy.com.

The Biology of Belief: Unleashing the Power of Consciousness, Matter, & Miracles by Bruce H. Lipton, (March, 2005), now Hay House, Inc.

The Essential Writings of Dr. Edward Bach: the Twelve Healers and Heal Thyself by Dr. Edward Bach, (2005), Random House.

The Field: The Quest for the Secret Force of the Universe, (2002), Harper Collins Publishers.

The Four Agreements: A Practical Guide to Personal Freedom by Don Miguel Ruiz, (November 7, 2007), Amber-Allan Publishing.

The Seat of the Soul by Gary Zukav, (1989), Simon and Schuster, Inc.

The Soul of Money: Reclaiming the Wealth of Our Inner Resources, by Lynne Twist and Teresa Barker, (2003), W.W. Norton and Co., London NY.

The Subtle Body: An Encyclopedia of Your Energetic Anatomy by Cyndi Dale, (February 1, 2009), Sounds True, Inc.

The Way of Liberation: A Practical Guide to Spiritual Enlightenment by Adyashanti (January 1, 2013), self-published.

The Yamas & Niyamas: Exploring Yoga's Ethical Practice by Deborah Adele, (2009), On-Word Books LLC.

Vibrational Medicine For the 21st Century, by Richard Gerber, M.D., (2001), HarperCollins Publishers.

Warrior of The Light: A Manual by Paulo Coelho, (2003), HarperCollins Publishers Inc.

Where Healing Waters Meet, Touching Mind & Emotion Through the Body, (1989), Station Hill Press.

You Can Heal Your Life by Louise Hay, (January 1, 1984), Hay House.

From the Clients

From Jackie Labarre's clients:

"Jackie LaBarre has been the one practitioner I go to when I need assistance. For the past year she has helped me by using Spiritual Mind Treatments which allow me to know the truth about any issue I'm facing. She has the understanding and inspiration to listen to my explanation of the problem such as a difficult relationship or health issue and assist me with identifying the causes and finding peace and joy."
~ Elaine Thorn

"It is with gratitude that I write a testimonial for Jackie LaBarre. I have had several opportunities to work with Jackie who has shared Spiritual Mind Treatments with me that have all been expansive experiences. Jackie has helped me recognize my own personal self worth and because she knows the truth of who I am, has helped me align and direct my thoughts in positive ways to know that I lack nothing and that all things are possible. Jackie has been an avenue to help me awaken to a greater sense of peace, clarity, harmony and prosperity because Jackie is a Love – filled Spirit that has a genuine presence of grace, joy and peace. Jackie is a beautiful, inspirational and compassionate individual, and it is through Jackie that I have been comforted and experienced healings as she has awakened my ever expanding potential to know the unlimited gift of God's love. Jackie has shown me that I am able to actively participate in the creation of my own life which has deepened my celebration of my life."
~ Virginia Worrell

From Enid Martinez's clients:

"I heard Enid Martinez speak at a Wellness conference and was immediately engaged by her passion, authenticity, and a rich mixture in total belief in what she was conveying. I then hired her to consult with me on my money management patterns with the intention to go forward with stronger tools to thrive financially and professionally. We embarked on one of the most meaningful growth experiences of my life, one in which Enid offered sage advice, on the spot intuitive visualization exercises, and an ongoing radiation to me that I was not only her client, but her purpose. In that process besides identifying strengths and areas I need to improve, she helped me see truths that can help me take great leaps going forward. She will be an amazing asset to your personal or business life if you hire her. I would be happy to elaborate on what she brings to the table if contacted."

~ B.L., New Jersey

"I found Enid's Money Coaching Process practical, creative and highly effective. Uncovering my primary limiting beliefs around finances and looking at those beliefs through the lens of archetypes has helped me develop powerful new ways of relating to how to create wealth and set financial goals. Accountability has shifted from being a burden to an exciting adventure; it's helping me create appropriate behaviors and actions unique to my financial situation. An alternative to (as well as complementary) traditional financial planning approaches, this process is FUN, enlightening, productive and an affordable, worthwhile investment in my financial future."

~ V.H., New Jersey

From Susan Lazar Hart's clients:

"I have so much gratitude for the contribution & expansion your class "A New Beginning with Right Relationship for You" gave to me & continues to gift me everyday. I attended the class in Australia at a time when I'd had enough of the heavy crap I'd created & was continuing to create with my relationship with myself, as I was holding onto a relationship that was NOT working for me at all. I watched many free recordings of your classes before choosing to come along as I find your honesty hilarious, I love your to the point awareness, no bullshit way of getting people out of our drama's/ stories (if we choose too). Your questions & clearings gave me the space to acknowledge my awareness of the heavy life I was

choosing, as it seemed easier to squash myself than to upset those who supposedly 'loved' me, although my body was in agony! I love that you live what you facilitate & I would highly recommend your class or private sessions to anyone, as it may very well be life changing as it has been & continues to be for me."

~ Tracey Thompson

"Over these three days I have fallen in love with my body and Susan Lazar Hart for being everything she is. She is one of the most beautiful people I have met. The level of awareness and ease she has is extra ordinary. Her humor and space of allowance adds a totally different dimension to her facilitation. Her ability to be aggressively present with every participant in the class is tremendous. Her willingness to contribute in all areas without a hesitation is such a beautiful invitation for everyone to step into the magic of possibilities. I don't have enough words to express the awareness that you have led me toward in your tender yet aggressive way. Delhi adores you and awaits to welcome you back soon with open arms and open hearts."

~ Bhavna Budhraja

From Dorinda Gay's clients:

"Through the years I've seen many spiritual people enter the healing and teaching arena only to exit a year or two later. Dorinda's practice continues to grow. Why? Because she's authentic."

~ Kathy O'Neill, Newburgh, NY

"Dorinda is a dedicated, knowledgeable, creative and joyful healer and teacher. Each session leaves me feeling better, more informed and uplifted. She hones in to the issue with intuition, guidance and integrity. I have also taken both Reiki and Energy Healing Classes with Dorinda. She has the gift of illuminating the strengths and talents of the student."

~ TM, Montrose, NY

From Lisa Crofton's clients:

"Attending one of Lisa's groups is more than a learning experience. Lisa's knowledge, wisdom and intuition guides the group to miraculous expansions. The modalities I have learned through Lisa has been a life changer. She has opened

my eyes to a new way of living. Thank you Lisa for giving me permission to live in my truth!"   ~ Sandi Liquindoli, Sole to Soul Healing

"Lisa genuinely supports each client to learn and grow in all areas of their lives for their highest good. She recognizes who you are immediately which so smoothly results in progressive and resourceful ideas for navigating life. Lisa has the incredible ability to put into words how I am feeling and what I want to express. so intuitive! Lisa is a beautiful example of a knowledgeable, loving being of light who is willing to show us all the way."

~ Sue Caterino, RN, Life Mastery Coach

From Anna Clayton's clients:

"In the past 5 years I have sought the help of numerous medical and alternative medicine practitioners in search of healing for the stubborn physical and emotional problems that long plagued me. While they were of help, it was only when I finally met Anna Clayton that I began to see and feel real, deep-rooted, and lasting healing. She is truly a "healer" in the full sense of that word. I have never met a person with so powerful a gift of healing, a gift that is not of this world. She is a treasure; she is also a lovely human being and it is a blessing to be in her presence. I have had many sessions with her and continue to do so, and after each session, not only do I feel better -- at the deepest level -- but I understand my self, my journey, and life with greater insight. I am extremely grateful for having been led to Anna Clayton."   ~ Franco M., Professor

"Anna is a remarkable healer! She has such a powerful, yet gentle, way of working. She treads lightly, asks about relationships and past issues with kindness and curiosity, and uses her intuition to hone in on the exact issue needing attention and healing. I love knowing that by working with her I am clearing out things that aren't serving me so that I can be my best possible self."

~ Deb E., Life Coach

From Barbra Richard's clients:

"Barbra and I met several years ago through a mutual friend who felt we shared the same devout love for animals. No one ever imagined that within a few months I would be faced with the heart-breaking task of helping my beloved Great Pyrenees and constant companion of 13-and-a-half years, Quinn, transition over the Rainbow Bridge. Barbra's spiritual and knowledgeable insight and gentle guidance helped both Quinn and I through this process of letting go of my best friend, losing, and then healing my heart. She created prayer sessions and conducted blessings for myself and Quinn in person as well as over the phone and made herself available whenever I needed her, day or night. Calls of support continued afterwards to see how I was healing with offerings of additional prayers, a visit to a farm animal sanctuary, and guidance as needed. And when the healing process was complete, she helped me expand my heart and life to another little soul, my sweet little Terrier, Meko. I am forever greatful for the love and compassion Barbra has gifted me throughout this immensely heart-wrenching time by providing me much needed comfort, healing, and peace of mind."

~ Deb Deboer, Owner of Deb's Dogcare Southington, CT

"Our connection with animals is a precious example of our spiritual selves. Barbra Richards has captured that connection and brought it to workshops designed to give us humans a clearer understanding of our world through our pets. Their instinctive natures are sometimes more on target than our own. During her workshops you have the sense that your animal friends are present and calling to you saying, "remember me." These pets pass through our lives but live on in our memories. Sometimes we need closure and sometimes just a remembrance of our dear friend. Barbra enhances that memory and creates an atmosphere of spirituality to show us our connection to the world. We are not separate but completely connected. Thank you Barbra for your guidance in this wild world."

~ Susan McKenzie

From Shareane Baff's clients:

"Shareane brings the best of everything to what she does! Whether it is designing her line of Goddess/Angel bracelets or consulting on Feng Shui, she is the consummate professional. Given her vast knowledge, keen intuition and positive energy she provides a safe place for others to change their lives for the better. Hav-

ing been one of Shareane's clients for almost 10 years, I have experienced dramatic changes in my life that I never dreamed possible. By sharing her love of life through the work that she does Shareane manifests a better world for all of us."

~ Jamie Gutierrez, Life coach

"It is Beyond words how my connection with Shareane Baff and Intentions Jewelry has changed my life personally and professionally. I call them my magic bracelets because they are Magical! I gave them out as a wedding gift and continue to give them for they have brought great blessings to all I have given! Shareane's bracelets have been an educational and a teaching tool for my spiritual intuitive development. Since being guided to purchase one I began my own direct connection with each of the Archangels, Ascended Masters, Gods or Goddesses that was channeled through it. Now that I have grown my own connection I have become a better spiritual teacher. Getting to know Shareane has been a true blessing in my life!!! She has become a mentor and a friend. It was definitely a divine connection!!! I am truly blessed and a better light worker since I met you at International Mediumship week many years ago in Omega."

~ Angel Eyes Dawn Marie

From Tami Reagor's clients:

"During our initial call Tami told me about the belief work that is Theta Healing and I was instantly intrigued. I scheduled my first session with her in January 2014, just a few days before my surgery. To say the first session was amazing is an understatement. I felt a surge of happiness, peace, and strength....I remember it clearly, and it helped prepare me for the road ahead. I truly believe the belief work Tami and I have done with ThetaHealing® had a significant impact on my recovery and treatment."   ~ Amy

"At a workshop with Tami, I asked that she help me lose the fear of driving on the highway. She asked me some questions, and gave me a healing! 2 days later, I wanted to see if ThetaHealing® made a difference for me, so I decided to attempt to drive home on I-95! I was wondering if the anxiety would build up again as I approached the ramp, but no it didn't-I felt calm and confident -I went up the ramp, got into the flow of traffic-no fear-and drove home. I was so happy! No problem, no anxiety."   ~ Roni L.

From MaryAnn Brouillard's clients:

"MaryAnn is an amazing, experienced, remarkable healer. She has the ability to get rid of negative energies & return them to a more balanced state. She has the capacity for doing such work in a kind, gentle, beautiful manner. I'm so grateful for the work she has done with me and respect her greatly."

~ Bernadette Grahn

"In the last seven years I have had the pleasure of getting to know MaryAnn not only on a professional level but on a personal level as well. What impresses me most about MaryAnn besides her overwhelming kindness, is how passionate she is to share her knowledge about health, nutrition, and energy healing. MaryAnn has such a deep rooted passion for spiritual wellness and healing, that she draws people in like a magnet. MaryAnn is one of those unique individuals that recognizes the human body as a spiritual being not a machine."

~ Michael P. Mahoney, V.P., Morgan Stanley Smith Barney

From Susan Draffan's clients:

"Working with flower, gem, and environmental essences has been healing and empowering in ways that I would not have believed possible. As a product of our mental, action oriented, dominion-over-nature society, I viewed healing as something formulaic to be captured. Deep seated fatigue, frustration, and alienation from Self due to years of coercing my body into wellness has softened. I have found myself relaxing into creative partnership and trust in the beneficence of the Universe. Access to this shimmering world wouldn't have been possible without Susan, a beautiful kind spirit equipped with deep ears, keen intelligence, and skillful ability to navigate and translate interconnected worlds with gentle communication and compassion. Her humility, grace, and integrity establish a potent background for exploration and transformation that is extraordinary, grounded, and practical. I trust her guidance and look up to her as a brilliant example of a shining spirit."

~ B.A., Center Conway NH

"I have had the honor of working with Susan for nearly a decade. In my opinion, the quality of her essence services and products is unsurpassed today. Over the years, my cats and I have successfully utilized her formulations for a wide range of concerns including illnesses, surgeries, hospitalizations, veterinary visits, rejuve-

nation, behavioral and social issues, travel, moving, space clearing, transition, bereavement, interspecies communication, spiritual expansion, and soul evolution. My tribe and I are always eager to use the essences Susan sends us. Each offers comfort and growth to body, mind, and soul. They are truly magical yet practical healing tools, both pleasurable to use and powerfully effective. I consider Susan to be a highly skilled and compassionate practitioner, as well as an intuitive artist who creates healing potions from the living world of nature. The essences she personally co-creates are simply spectacular. I highly recommend her, and her work."

~ R. K., Stonington

From Karen Lemieux's clients:

"I received an Intuitive Healing session, and attained my Reiki 1 practitioner certificate from Karen. She is an effective teacher and is exceptionally perceptive and sensitive. I continue to participate in her weekly Kundalini Yoga classes which are a powerful means of healing through energy, sound and postures. Working with Karen has helped me to continue to heal from various issues I struggle with especially related to loss. Through Intuitive Healing and Reiki I have embraced what we all know deep within ourselves, but have forgotten. That is, we are always connected to the source of all life and healing, and therefore we know how to heal ourselves."

~ Elaine Webber, MSN, RN

"It was my good fortune to have Karen facilitate an Intuitive Healing Session. At all times I felt the gentleness emanating from Karen as she guided me towards my own self-reflective journey. I felt an innate sense of safety to share my vulnerability in my healing process. I experienced a shift and release in blocked energies which created space for new good in my life. I would highly recommend Karen for anyone who needs guidance to help propel them forward in their journey."

~ Lisa Barrett. M.A.

From Andrea Frasier's clients:

"Andrea came into my life a few years ago introducing her magical touch of energy work after a yoga class. I became interested in her healing powers both emotionally and physically so I consequently became certified in Reiki I and II

146

under her instruction and guidance. After experiencing several Reiki sessions with Andrea and the abovementioned certifications I realized the powers of self-healing and Reiki as a tool in managing daily living with a more positive outlook. (The sky isn't falling!) As for the most noticeable physical change/healing Andrea has done for me was eliminating the pain and discomfort I had for some time in my right hip. I am now pain free! I feel blessed and honored to be a part of Andrea's spiritual and energy awakening she has been called upon to share with others."

~ Lynda Miklos, CT

"I took Andrea Frasier's Reiki level I, II and III over a year span. I have to be honest, I am a changed person inside and out. Some things that have changed in my life after taking reiki I noticed are I am a much calmer, caring individual. Reiki has helped me become more aware of other's feelings, as well as my own feelings and how to keep them in a positive, caring place. Working with Andrea is like working with an angel that has so much love, trust and abundance. You can't help but fall in love with her great personality and her commitment to her work. I would highly recommend taking Reiki with Andrea."

~ Cathy Rivera, CT

From Dan Lupacchino's clients:

"I have been working with Dan since August 2014 for a variety of spiritual healing practices and learning. For me, what I liked about Dan immediately was his energy which is so full of life, compassion, and understanding. He has an excellent work ethic and he is truly dedicated to his clients and the work that he does. I feel extremely blessed to have Dan as my spiritual teacher and healer in my life. Dan is truly inspiring and I strongly recommend his services to anyone who is hungry for knowledge, going through a spiritual journey, or who simply just wants to connect with their higher divine self."

~ A.I.

"I started working with Dan in the Fall of 2012, originally seeking him out for massage therapy. Our work together has grown to include many styles of massage therapy and energy healing modalities. Dan's caring, and compassionate attention to detail, as well as his intuitive ability to suggest the best type of treatment for you on a given day; make a session with him meaningful and worthwhile. I feel

better physically and emotionally after an appointment with Dan. His skill and talent, that includes infusing energy and aromatherapy into his massages, is something that you need to experience for yourself!" ~ I.K.

From Lauren Brandstadter's clients:

"I am an old athlete with a high stress job. I was introduced to Lauren more than two years ago to help me with management of my stress and joint pain. Since then I have sessions with Lauren on a nearly monthly basis. I have found her to be the best massage therapist I have ever worked with in over thirty years! Lauren's experience and broad knowledge of technique and theory make her work incomparable. An example: without mentioning any issues, within five minutes on the table Lauren has identified the "problem" areas and begins her work. Besides her skill, Lauren's positive attitude re-enforces your resolve to live a healthy life." ~ William R. Hansen

"Lauren is the real deal. She gives 100% of herself when treating someone. Her expertise has been honed by years of practice and is ever expanded upon because of an incessant desire to be the best for her patients, her friends and herself. She sensitively applies her wisdom in ways that open disrupted energy channels, restoring balance, reducing and/or eliminating pain and bringing mental ease. What a gift she has been in my life! I am grateful and can hardly wait for my next session." ~ Conrad Szymkowicz

From Jill Myruski's clients:

"Each massage with Jill is a gift to my total wellness. I walk in feeling, "not so great" and always leave with both a physical and mental sense of wellness, calm, relaxation and happiness. Jill's energy/massage work has made a total difference in my quality of life. I can feel the swirling, thriving movement of energy in my body well after my massage." ~ Kathleen Felix

"Jill Myruski has been working with me for about a year now with great results. I have been battling undiagnosed muscle and soft tissue pain for many years. I've had epidurals, cortisone shots, taken daily NSAID pain relievers, over the counter pain medication, done physical therapy numerous times, seen Rheumatologists,

148

orthopedic surgeons for consultations, chiropractors… you name it. Since meeting with Jill on a regular basis, my symptoms have either stopped or been greatly reduced. Her counseling and insight as well as her healing therapies have changed my outlook as well as eliminated much of the day to day pain and frustration that comes along with it! She clearly has a knack to "see" where there is an issue and go directly at it to either disperse the bad energy or get the good energy flowing. Life changing! She has given me considerable hope as well as opened my mind to a whole body approach to my health."   ~ Kaye Jeronowitz

From Cynthia Haas' clients:

"Cynthia is a master in her art of healing. Her loving, tender, empathetic and nurturing spirit is what healed me physically and emotionally. She has an unmatched, radiant energy that makes you feel grounded just by being in the same room as her. She is not just a massage therapist; she is a healer." ~Taylor Itsell

"I was recommended to Cynthia for massage. The treatments were the best I've encountered but learning about so many more aspects of living a healthier life I had to return to further advance my education. Her passion, knowledge and continuing advancement for all things homeopathic and healing techniques are just astounding. She is on the leading edge and a true rarity for health and general wellness. I would credit my positive lifestyle changes and thirst for my growing knowledge one of my great resources."   ~ Brett Bigelow

From Diane April's clients:

"Diane April is more than just a wonderful reflexologist: she's a healer. While I do not consider myself much of a spiritual person, I felt a very strong connection to Diane from the moment I met her. When I'm with her, I know she's treating all of me. Several years ago, I had my gallbladder removed. During my recovery, I saw Diane often and I'm convinced that she played an integral role in my healing process. I called her my "antioxidant". Diane is equally caring as she is professional. If you are looking to be treated holistically, you need to try Diane. She's the real deal!"   ~ Rhonda Markman, Personal Trainer, Nutritionist

149

"As an avid consumer of body work I have experienced many methodologies and even learned and practiced a few along the way. Diane's reflexology sessions were among the most relaxing and calming I have ever experienced. She left me feeling balanced and grounded and as I heard someone very wise say, "I felt as if I had a massage from the inside out." The energy coming out of her hands was intensely comforting, healing and loving. Pure Magic!" ~ Rebecca Hill Bruder

From Jiayuh Chyan's clients:

"I was stuck and holding onto a lot of things but I was at a loss as to how to release it. I received two Arcturian Healing sessions from Jiayuh. I have to say that I think these two sessions were the most powerful healing sessions I've received to date! I felt lighter, content in a way that I hadn't experienced in a long time. Jiayuh changed my life and helped me find myself again." ~ Carrie

"I have had issues with my jaw, shoulder and elbow for quite some time and have tried different modalities to relieve them with only temporary short term relief. The healing sessions with Jiayuh was not only physical but I was also able to release the emotional reasons behind what was going on. These sessions were one of the best experiences with body work/ healing I have ever had. I would highly recommend Jiayuh." ~ Chris

From Cara Sax's clients:

"Cara is a healer. She heals with her heart, her head and her actions. I've been fortunate to have taken her classes for the last decade and undoubtedly, I walk out of her classes feeling better physically and spiritually. There is a warmth, an understanding and a relatedness about her that allows anyone to feel connected and part of a whole. Intuitive and kind, her presence is always greeted with smiles and appreciation for her helpful healing." ~ Sharyse Eisinger Ph.D.

"I am a dance teacher, therapist and social worker, and have known Cara for approximately ten years, first taking class alongside her, then taking her class for the past four years or so. Cara's class is consistently awesome EVERY time. She hits the right balance of challenge and compassion in each session. She is encour-

aging, warm and caring, providing a well-structured class that I have come to love. Most people that come in to take her class become "lifers"! During her classes, there is a feeling that every person in the room is valued. She has the innate ability to address a room full of practitioners at a variety of levels, and make all persons feel that their needs are addressed. As a dance teacher, it is imperative that I keep my body aligned, and my mind receptive to creativity. Without a doubt, her class has allowed me to stay aligned, and helped keep me open to the creative process."

~ Tina Maxwell, LMSW

About the Authors

Jackie LaBarre, RScP

Jackie LaBarre is the owner of Conscious Healing Center located in Bethel, CT. As an engineer with a diverse background, she has worked at large corporations in a variety of management positions. In her leadership positions, Jackie developed her skills to listen deeply and help people find their true calling in life. After leaving the corporate world, she trained as a massage therapist and became the owner of her massage school. It was at this time she was introduced to the spiritual principles and practices which she used to create and develop her successful massage school. Jackie is now a Licensed Spiritual Practitioner with Centers for Spiritual Living practicing through the Connecticut Center for Spiritual Living and also a spiritual life coach in her Conscious Healing Center. She has recently become a certified Dream Builder Coach with Mary Morrissey's Life Mastery Institute. For more information, visit www.chctransformation.com or email: jackie@chctransformation.com.

Enid Martinez, CMC®

Enid Martinez is a Certified Money Coach (CMC)® and Spiritual Counselor. She is also a former International Private Banker. Enid skillfully integrates these disciplines into powerful tools to help others build more fulfilling lives. Enid effectively guides and assists others, through practical and simple ways, to become more aware about their relationship to money and themselves. Most importantly, she assists and guides others from a place of non-judgment to make changes in their lives and money behaviors. Her ability to see the full spectrum of a client's situation aids in getting to the root of a client's challenge and allows for true, effective solutions. Enid guides others to actively live the lives they dream and experience financial freedom. Enid's other passion is doing healing work with animals, both wild and domestic, including assisting with transitioning during their dying process. She also teaches classes on Spirituality, Intuition and Money. Enid received her training and certification from The Money Coaching Institute, a coaching training organization located in Northern California. She also completed 60 credits at Holos University Graduate Seminary in the field of Energy Medicine and Spirituality in which she has over ten years of experience. She earned an MBA in Finance from Rutgers University, and is certified in Basic Hypnotherapy. Enid can be contacted at enid@affluentawareness.com or visit her website at affluentawareness.com.

Susan Lazar Hart, MFA

Susan Lazar Hart transforms the way people experience relationships and intimacy. As the Executive Creator of Right Relationship for You™ (RRFY), she travels the world offering Right Relationship™ classes and training her global network of RRFY™ Facilitators. With her straight-forward approach and her irreverent sense of humor, Susan combines the tools of Access Consciousness™ with her experience as a wife, mother, artist, life coach and relationship counselor to inspire people around the world to search for new realities in every relationship. Susan holds a CFMW from Access Consciousness, a Professional and Personal Coaching Certification from Concordia University, as well as a Masters in Fine Arts Degree. www.susanlazarhart.com

Dorinda Gay

Dorinda Gay, founder of From The Universe To You, Inc., describes herself as an energy intuitive whose inner voice, along with Spirit's, guides her clearly to live and love deeply on this planet. She maintains an active private practice in Croton on Hudson, NY and serves as an energy and space clearing consultant to homes and businesses across the country. She is building an Energy Teaching program to assist others in bringing forth their own healing gifts. Exploring the mysterious wonder of Earth drives her to lead journeys in magical Sedona. She considers joy, connection and play vital to living well. DorindaGay.com, Fromtheuniversetoyou.com.

Lisa Crofton, RMT

Lisa Crofton is a Spiritual Intuitive, Life Mastery Coach and Soul Realignment Practitioner as well as a Reiki Master Teacher. She is co-founder of the Bloom Life Mastery Coach Training School in Southington, CT and runs Lotus Moon Studios, LLC, a holistic healing center. Lisa offers unique Intuitive Life Mastery Coaching for private clients and groups as well as online teaching programs and retreats. Combining 30 years of entrepreneurial experience, holistic healing training certifications and tapping into her own intuitive methods, Lisa guides others to discover their soul's blueprint and follow the unique path that lights their life on fire! www.lotusmoonstudios.com. lotusmoonreiki@gmail.com.

Anna Clayton, MA, LMFT

Anna Clayton is an Intuitive Healer with her own unique healing gift, Mother's Milk Divine Mother Energy. She is also a licensed psychotherapist, a certified herbalist and shamanic healer, and a certified holistic health and nutrition coach. She combines this expertise with her psychic healing abilities to create Transformational Healing. She is able to clear issues below the level of consciousness, at the karmic level and even the genetic level. She offers individual sessions in person and at a distance. To contact Anna or to book a session, please see her website, www.InsightfulTransformation.com

Barbra Richards, RScP, VIP, AC

Barbra Richards and her Animal and Nature Ministry, Paws, Prayers 'n People, was established after becoming an Animal Chaplain and a Credentialed Animal Bereavement Facilitator through the Emerson Theological Institute's Humane Division in 2012. Late Summer of 2015, she was licensed as a Spiritual Prayer Practitioner through the Connecticut Center for Spiritual Living. She provides services and celebrations for humans and their animal companions along the continuum of life. She lives in a small cottage overlooking a lake surrounded by nature and her three animal companions, Smudgy, Kismet and Charlotte, writing and offering inspiration and healing to humans and their animal companions. Contact Barbra at pawsprayersnpeople@gmail.com or www.pawsprayersnpeople.com.

Shareane Baff

Shareane Baff has been a student of spirituality for what seems like her whole life. From as early as 8 years old, Shareane can remember hearing her angel's wisdom as she would pray for guidance. It was then that she developed an intimate relationship with the world of spirit. Shareane went on to graduate from the BTB Feng Shui Masters Training Program, and has had the privilege to study under Grand Master Lin Yun, among other master teachers and internationally recognized authorities on Feng Shui. Shareane is also the owner and creator of Intentions Jewelry. This unique collection combines Shareane's knowledge of Feng Shui and her trance mediumship skills allowing her to infuse the finest crystal with divine energy. Shareane works closely with and has developed a bracelet line for world renowned spiritual medium, James Van Praagh. Shareane is available for Soul to Soul consultations, Bracelet consultations, teaching and speaking engagements, and Feng Shui consultations. To learn more about Shareane visit www.intentionsjewelry.com.

Tami Reagor, CHHC

Tami Reagor is a Holistic Health & Soul Coach, Advanced Theta-Healing® practitioner and instructor, Certified Holistic Health Coach, author, speaker and teacher. Based in Walllingford, Connecticut, she is committed to spreading the word about how a change in your thoughts and perspective can change your world from blah to awesome! Tami has written and published her first book: Unleash Your Inner Tiger: Strength, Beauty & Power. Tami privately coaches her clients and conducts workshops and seminars to teach and help people integrate this new way of looking at the world into their lives. Contact Tami at tami@wellbeingis.com or visit www.wellbeingis.com.

MaryAnn Brouillard, RN, CHHP

MaryAnn Brouillard developed 'SoulRepair' Energy Healing, a symphony of hands on healing techniques which supports the body's natural state of energetic balance. Working with the energy centers (Chakras), channeling Divine, Universal and Earth Energy, to restore one's life force to optimal well-being of the Mind, Body and SoulRepair. She is a Registered Nurse with a diverse career in adult medicine and alternative healing modalities and is pursuing a Master of Arts Degree in Integrative Health and Healing at The Graduate Institute, and has a BSN in Nursing at the University of Bridgeport. She attended three years of study at the Center for Healing and became certified in Transformational Energy Healing and its Teaching Program, a Reiki practitioner, Holistic Health Practitioner (CHHP) certified by the American Association of Drugless Practitioners (AADP), and member of American Holistic Nurses Association. Contact MaryAnn at Soulrepair11@gmail.com.

Susan Draffan, MA

Initiated into the unseen realms in childhood, Susan Draffan maintains relationships with her multidimensional plant, creature, faery and cosmic allies in service to unifying the living worlds. She is a nature and animal intuitive and vibrational essence specialist who helps clients of all species awaken to their magnificence, purpose and divinity. In her practice, Susan draws on skills from her advanced academic degrees, previous career as a diagnostic medical clinician and counselor, holistic healing arts training, and Celtic spirituality studies. She is currently developing a line of essences in the luminous Ojai Valley, where she resides with her human and feline family. Contact Susan at info@ShiningSpirits.net, or visit www.ShiningSpirits.net.

Karen Lemieux, LCSW

Karen Lemieux is a Licensed Clinical Social Worker, Spiritual Practitioner, Intuitive Healer, Kundalini Yoga and Reiki Master Teacher. Her life's work has been to understand what causes and what relieves suffering on the individual and global level. As a trauma specialist with expertise in child sexual abuse and war trauma, Karen has helped thousands find their way back to optimal health and well- being restoring harmony and balance in the mental, physical, emotional, spiritual and soul body. Karen views all of life as sacred and empowers us to remember that we are our own healers. www.karenlemieux.net.

Andrea Frasier, RMT

Andrea Frasier is a down to Earth spiritual teacher and guide. She is a compassionate Reiki master teacher, transformational coach, author, and certified crystal healer. Her innate ability to connect with clients and help them find their inner-healer, sets her apart in the field of energy healing. Andrea believes that we all have a healer within us, and she is determined to help others find it! She holds a Master's degree in education, is a National Board certified teacher, Reiki master teacher, and angel card reader with life-long studies in energy healing, chakra balancing, crystal healing, connecting with angels, A Course in Miracles, and Ho'oponopono. Her healing methods include Reiki, including the higher, more ethereal vibration of Lightarian Reiki, crystals, and angel therapy. She provides useful insights and tips about all of these topics on her blog at www.AndreaFrasier.com

Dan Lupacchino, LMT

Dan Lupacchino is a gifted healer, reader and teacher. Having started his holistic training at the age of 16, he has built his holistic practice over the last eleven years to include Massage Therapy, Energy Healing and Intuitive work. He is a Licensed Massage Therapist, Medical Intuitive, Spiritual Counselor, Master Healer and Integrated Energy Therapy (IET®) Master Instructor, recently being named a 2014 IET® Top Instructor. The scope of his class topics includes healing, meditation, metaphysical practices and spirituality. Dan practices and teaches at The Healing in Harmony Center in Glastonbury, CT and has published an article on Integrated Energy Therapy ® in "The Door Opener Magazine." www.integrativemassageworks.com, dan@integrativemassageworks.com.

Lauren Brandstadter, LMT

Lauren Brandstadter received her Bachelors in Communications from Iona College in 1988, and Massage Therapy Certification from The Swedish Institute in 1992. Formerly a publicist for Psychology Today, Mother Earth News, and the Weider Publications (Shape, Men's Fitness, Muscle & Fitness and Flex), she has been a contributing writer for Holistic Primary Care, a newsletter for Alternative Medical Practitioners. Lauren is in private practice, licensed in New York and Hawaii. She has studied and practiced Medical, Western, Eastern, Polynesian, Energetic, Emotional and Spiritual techniques over the course of her 26-year career. As a Master, she combines these techniques for maximum healing results. Lauren lived off the grid in Easter Island, which transformed her as a healer, and human. She is an Aromatherapist, a Maker of Remedies, a Universal Life Church Reverend, and a medium. Contact Lauren at lbrandstadter@gmail.com or www.PacificWindsWellness.com.

Jill Myruski, LMT

Jill Myruski earned a Bachelor's of Science in Business administration at SUNY New Paltz in 1982 and graduated from The Connecticut Center for Massage Therapy in 1996. She is licensed in Massage Therapy in Connecticut and New York and has been in private practice for more then 20 years as an intuitive Massage Therapist and Healer. While in massage school, Jill discovered she had a gift for feeling energy and a knack for applying holistic principals in her work with people. This resulted in many outcomes of solving painful issues her clients were having in their bodies by using hands on methods of massage, energy work and intuitive guidance. Jill discovered that she could feel a vibration where ever there is blocked energy in and around the body. She created a technique called Vibrational Release, that she uses to balance our human energy fields. Ever inspired by natural medicine and the necessity of it in our world, Jill has added Health Coaching, Holistic Skin Care and Aromatherapy to her practices, www.liveyourtransformation.com and www.bewellandbeautiful.net.

Cynthia Haas, BS, LMT

Cynthia Haas, is a Massage Therapist, Kundalini Yoga Teacher, and Aromatherapist and has always been interested in health and nutrition. She taught herself yoga from a book when she was 21 years old. She enrolled in massage school and graduated from the Ann Arbor Institute of Massage Therapy in 1996. While in school, she was introduced to essential oils and began experiencing a major difference in her massage practice and her life when using therapeutic grade oils. She wrote a course in Essential Oils for the massage school. She is a teacher and advocate for taking responsibility, not being victims to disease. Cynthia loves to see people get healthy by teaching them about essential oils, how to make changes in their diet, teaching easy breathing techniques, ways to de-stress and more. Contact Cynthia at cjhaas9@comcast.net.

Diane April

Diane April is a nationally certified Reflexologist. Her holistic training began in 1999 when she took her first Reiki workshops. To maintain her passionate connection to the natural world, Diane studied Horticultural Therapy at the New York Botanical Garden. In 2003 she trained at the Laura Norman Reflexology Center and then graduated from the Institute for Integrative Nutrition. Diane maintains a private practice in Westchester County, New York; she consults for Hospice and Palliative Care of Westchester, and volunteers at the local Ronald McDonald House. When she isn't working, Diane can be found playing in nature, experimenting in the kitchen, or hanging out at home with her beloved Buster the cat. dianeapril23@gmail.com.

Jiayuh Chyan, MS

Jiayuh Chyan is a Council and Certified Teacher of The Akashic Network, a Certified Healing Touch Practitioner, and an Arcturian Healing Practitioner. Jiayuh completed certified teacher training at the Center for Akashic Studies. She is also the New Haven Chapter president of the Holistic Chamber of Commerce and a retired actuary. Jiayuh holds a Master's Degree in Applied Mathematics – Actuarial Science from The University of Illinois at Urbana-Champaign. Jiayuh is sincere, genuine and compassionate. Her strength is the ability to speak from her heart, connect with your heart, see the divine light in you, and help to guide you on your path. Jiayuh's services include Akashic Records Certification Classes, Akashic Records Consultation, Arcturian Healing, Sacred Geometry Healing, and Healing Touch. Contact Jiayuh Chyan at jiayuh@jiayuhchyan.com or www.jiayuhchyan.com.

Cara Sax, ERYT 200, HHC

Cara Sax is a certified yoga teacher, fitness trainer and holistic health counselor. She is the owner of Elevate Yoga Studio in Cortlandt Manor, New York. She has been in the field of health and healing for over thirty years. Her Bachelor's degree in Exercise Science gives her a strong foundation and excellent understanding of the physical body when she creates her vinyasa style flow yoga classes. Through her blog, www.perfectbalancewith-cara.com, Cara shares her thoughts, ideas, and advice on how to use the tools passed down from the ancient philosophy of yoga to deal with present day challenges. She is certified in Yoga Trance Dance and has developed her own style of YogaDance which she often teaches at her bi-annual yoga retreats in the Catskills. Other certifications include prenatal yoga and holistic health counseling.